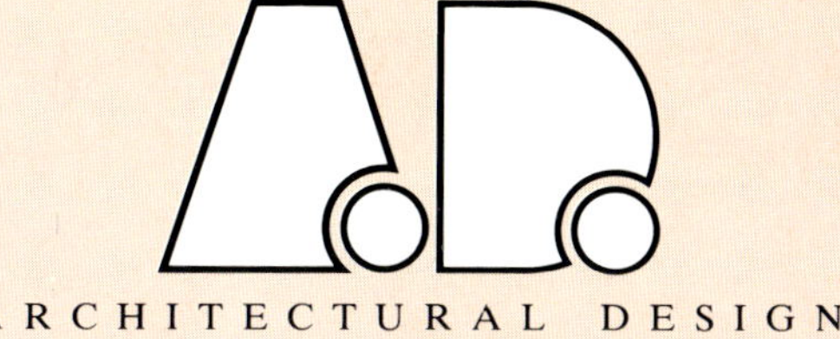

A.D.
ARCHITECTURAL DESIGN
Vol 58 No 9/10-1988

Editorial Offices: 42 Leinster Gardens, London W2 Telephone: 01-402 2141 Subscriptions: 7/8 Holland Street London W8

EDITOR
Dr Andreas C Papadakis
PRODUCTION EDITOR: Pamela Johnston DESIGNED BY: Andrea Bettella, Mario Bettella
ASSISTANT EDITOR: Natasha Edwards ADVERTISING: Sheila de Vallée SUBSCRIPTIONS MANAGER: Hedy Kraemer
CONSULTANTS: Catherine Cooke, Dennis Crompton, Terry Farrell, Kenneth Frampton
Charles Jencks, Heinrich Klotz, Leon Krier, Robert Maxwell, Demetri Porphyrios, Colin Rowe, Derek Walker

ROBERT ADAM, WORCESTER COLLEGE, OXFORD, GARDEN ELEVATION

IMITATION AND INNOVATION

MUSEUM FÜR KUNSTHANDWERK, FRANKFURT, DETAIL

MEIER AND THE MODERN TRADITION

Charles Jencks

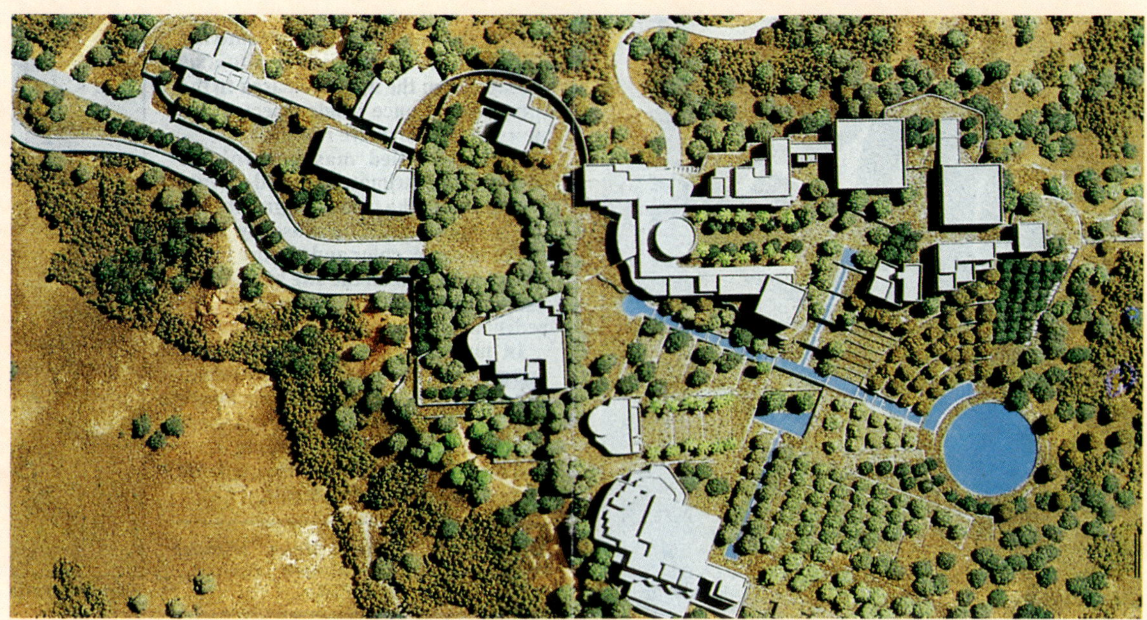

J PAUL GETTY CENTER, BRENTWOOD, CALIFORNIA, MODEL

Sigfried Giedion subtitled his polemical history of Modern Architecture, *Space Time and Architecture*, 'the growth of a new tradition', and he adjusted the fifth edition of 1967 to recent developments, the change to a sculptural freedom. The work of Jørn Utzon, Kenzo Tange and Fumihiko Maki and the Brazilians showed where the 'third generation' of Modernists were going: 'architecture is approaching sculpture and sculpture is approaching architecture'. Or, as he

formalised the new-found permissiveness of this generation: 'the right of expression above pure function'. Since then, of course, we have had the fourth and fifth generation of Modernists – this tradition speeds up its breeding cycles like everything else – and if Giedion were alive today he would, no doubt, include a key chapter in the latest version of the New Testament called 'Richard Meier and the Mastery of Light and Geometry'. Meier fits into the canonic line of Modernist development as smoothly and comfortably as Bramante continued 50 years of Renaissance practice. In both cases an architect is assuming and extending a well-known language at a very high level of creation and execution and in both cases there is a certain begrudging admiration on the part of contemporaries.

Raphael and Michelangelo were impressed by Bramante's undoubted virtuosity, but they found it a little tiring, the brilliant solution of old problems. The complex situation of a pluralist architecture today displaces these same feelings about a host of traditions and many contemporaries are now bored with the Post-Modernism of Michael Graves, the revivalism of Quinlan Terry, the High-Tech of Rogers and the Modernism of Meier, to name a few of the major movements which have become institutionalised. That is, many people are simply bored by *any* tradition, even if it's done well and extended.

I mention this pervasive ennui because it has coloured appreciation of Richard Meier's work from the very beginning. When his Smith House was first published in the late 60s and *The Five*

Architects soon after, several American and European critics reacted against what they took to be a devalutation, distortion or deconstruction of the Modernists' social message: 'Le Corbusier ÷ la Mode, or Revolution for the Sell of It', as Peter Papademetriou wrote in *Architectural Design*. The translation of the white architecture from social housing into private temples for the *nouveaux riches* was considered reactionary, and by some a betrayal.

Such views, while understandable, missed some important qualities of Meier's work as well as a key ambiguity of the Modern Movement. As Adolf Loos proclaimed (and Tom Wolfe was later to argue) Modernism has been built essentially for and by the bourgeoisie, no matter how much its ideology has favoured mass housing and a working class, and machine, aesthetic. Without the *nouveaux riches*, just as without industrialisation, Modernism would be dead. A new class of patrons intent on showing its cultural acumen is essential for its continual well-being and if there is a basic dynamic to Modernism it rests on one fundamental fact: for 200 years there has been modernisation, development, a progressive technology and economic growth. Both cultural Modernism and economic capitalism depend on the dynamic of innovation, the shock of the new, the destruction of the old.

This is what gives Meier's work such poignancy and pathos: it is 'new/old' like Bramante's architecture must have seemed in 1500, and also 'capitalist/socialist' in its overtones, like so much

MUSEUM FUR KUNSTHANDWERK, FRANKFURT, PERSPECTIVE DRAWING

current art. Building luxury dream houses with a workers' vernacular may seem a paradox to Tom Wolfe, but to anyone who watches *Dynasty* and *Dallas* it's a normal event. The Modernist aesthetic lends itself to class and probity as readily as did Palladian architecture in the 18th century and it is only sentimentality for the 20s, when the Heroic Period and socialist ideology were in their prime, which keeps us from acknowledging this truth.

Meier's architecture, like so much Neo-Modernism, makes an art out of this quandary. It takes readily available industrial materials – particularly the porcelain-enamel panel – and turns them into ideal, luxurious tokens fit for a king, or at least a museum committee. The abstraction and geometry appeal to the intellectual (another class of Meier admirers) and of course the professionals (which is one reason he received the Gold Medal in 1988). And there is also the *populus* which is impressed by all the glittering white promise of a shining new instrument (the Atlanta Museum *is* a popular public space), so the work does indeed cut across different groups and tastes by using industrial materials in a fabulously pristine way.

What does it add to Giedion's 'modern tradition'? Among other things a delightful repetition of the grid motif used at different scales and in various materials, an idea of Josef Hoffmann played at a new tempo; the skew and shifted grids leading to ever more sharp and dissonant angled planes – 45 degrees, 22½, 12 and finally the 3½ degree skew at Frankfurt. These result in exquisite intersections and a spatial dissonance which keeps one moving. Then there's the new version of Baroque light rebounding not through Le Corbusier's double-height spaces but four-storey sections. And the fragmented piano-shapes and broken-up Purist forms, equally indebted to Corb's synthetic Cubism, but more complex, dissonant and picturesque – the reason Meier was termed 'Post-Johnson-Corb' in the 60s.

Such fractures and collisions signify 'imperfect perfection', 'unclear clarity', 'irrational rationality' – the oxymoronic figures and meanings which destabilise the certainty of the Modernist white-aesthetic. And here lies the essence of Meier's contribution to the 'new tradition', to Late-Modernism or Neo-Modernism (I would use the terms interchangeably in his case): it is the note of celebration amidst a questioning doubt, an affirmation of the 'Modern project', of reason and the Enlightenment, at the same time as it's a sensuous denial of the

WESTCHESTER HOUSE, NEW YORK STATE, VIEW FROM SOUTHWEST

dogmatism of the ideology through the play with sculptural form and light. Those who want to find in Meier's work an intellectual ordering – the abstract distinction between public and private, geometry and nature, necessity and freedom – will continue to be transported by this abstract language, because it is played with a brilliance that would have pleased Le Corbusier. It won't please everyone – no architecture does in an age of pluralism and where the limits of abstraction are known. But unlike so much Modernism today, Meier's is kept taut and fresh, reminding us that architectural languages don't die, but rather that certain architects get tired of using them.

———— * ————

'The importance of Meier's contribution does not reside in the undoubted brilliance of his architectural form, but in the urban implications of his larger set-pieces. In this sense perhaps, he is not only the last Modernist, but also, paradoxically, perhaps the last European, in the Jamesian sense. Thus as the Dutch and other Europeans Americanise themselves at break-neck pace and lose all control over that which Wright called the "cause conservative", we have much to learn from him.' Kenneth Frampton

Richard Meier was awarded the 1988 Royal Gold Medal for Architecture. Drawings, photographs and models of Meier's recent Westchester House in New York State and the City Hall and Library in The Hague are currently on show at the 9H Gallery in London, whilst his Museum für Kunsthandwerk (Museum for the Decorative Arts) in Frankfurt is featured in the exhibition 21 Canonic Architects *organised by the Academy Group at the Deutsches Architekturmuseum for the duration of October. Academy Editions will be publishing an important fully illustrated monograph on Richard Meier in July 1989. Concentrating on his recent works and edited and designed in close collaboration with the architect, it features an essay by Kenneth Frampton, who argues that Richard Meier's greatest contribution has not been his private houses but his recent designs in Europe at Ulm and The Hague where he is forced to respond to questions of urban form and context, and extracts from a series of previously unpublished discussions that have taken place over a number of years between Meier and Charles Jencks and which reveal his philosophy of design and method of work.*

L TO R: *DINERS' PARADISE*, 1988, INSTALLATION DETAIL; HEIDE WARLAMIS, SALT AND PEPPER SET, 1986

Design Heute
Volker Fischer
Prestel Verlag, Munich, 1988
325pp, b&w and col ills, paper,

This weighty and scholarly catalogue, written principally by Volker Fischer, with essays by Volker Albus, Jochen Gros and Matteo Thun, accompanies an exhibition held at the Deutsches Architekturmuseum, Frankfurt, from May to August 1988.

The account, in German, is museological and academic, with classification of objects into categories such as Canonical, Minimalist, High-Tech, Trans-High-Tech, Post-Modern, Archetypal, Micro-Architecture and Banal Design. The work is excellently illustrated with images which run the gamut from Thonet in 1900 to recent work, and enlists much of the available taxonomy of object-based culture.

Museum accounts are always at risk from rigid classification, and not all the neat pigeon-holes fit the designers. By no means all the products named as Micro-Architecture are such: Stanley Tigerman's and Hans Hollein's silverware sets for Alessi are cases in point, and would be better included in the Post-Modern section. Frank Gehry's chair, which is informed by Deconstructivism nestles rather too tritely under Post-Modern. Freer flow between such groupings would have benefitted the account. This catalogue, as one might expect, is heavily inflected towards German work, with as yet unproven talents such as that of Heide Warlamis having more space than Arata Isozaki; Berghof, Landes and Rang's secondary Post-Modern furniture gets almost equal billing with Michael Graves' superior and primary Post-Modern work. The fact remains that German design lags behind Italian and American contemporary work; given that the days of the Bauhaus or Ulm are over, the nationalistic slant of the catalogue suggests a propagandist intent. The section on Dieter Rams' excellent design is for example, more thorough than that on Alchimia and Memphis. Imbalance is also seen in the space accorded the *Made in Venice* lamps rivalling that given to the Aldo Rossi work to which their authors, Vendruscolo and Gerard, are indebted.

One of the best essays is by the designer Matteo Thun, who coined the design concept 'Baroque Bauhaus', and has written a provocative account of Neo-Baroque for this catalogue.

It is surprising to find in such a museum-based catalogue few biographical details, or even the dates of birth of the designers, many of whom are as yet little known. Conversely, objects are dated and even measured with fastidious accuracy. Such a dearth of information about designers is rather surprising and highly irritating, but then, museums have never been particularly renowned for their concern with the living.

The other obvious limitation is that the exhibition only covers that which can be easily shown in O M Ungers' relatively small museum; anything bigger than furniture, for example the motor car, is excluded from the account. Object based works of this sort can only present a partial view of design history: in fact the catalogue is far more about the decorative arts and domestic items that it is about design. This *Schatzkammer* approach is exemplified by the installation *Diners' Paradise* at the exhibition, with over 100 domestic items, none much over a foot in height, on display.

The catalogue is, none the less, a welcome contribution to the history of three-dimensional decorative art and design. The exhibition remains to date the best demonstration of design in the age of pluralism, and despite the aforementioned limitations, reveals the widening paths available to design practitioners at the end of the 1980s.
Michael Collins

Further Books Received

The Rietveld Schröder House
Paul Overy, et al
Butterworth, Guildford, 1988
127pp, b&w and col ills, cloth, £25

The biography of Gerrit Rietveld's small simple open-plan house in Utrecht, that has become a paradigm of Modernism. The house has recently been restored and is now open to the public. The book includes an interview with Mrs Schröder who commissioned the house and who talks about her role in its design and an essay by Bertus Mulder, architect responsible for its restoration.

Understanding Modern Architecture
Patrick Nuttgens
Unwin Hyman, London, 1988
220pp, b&w ills, cloth, £ 14.95

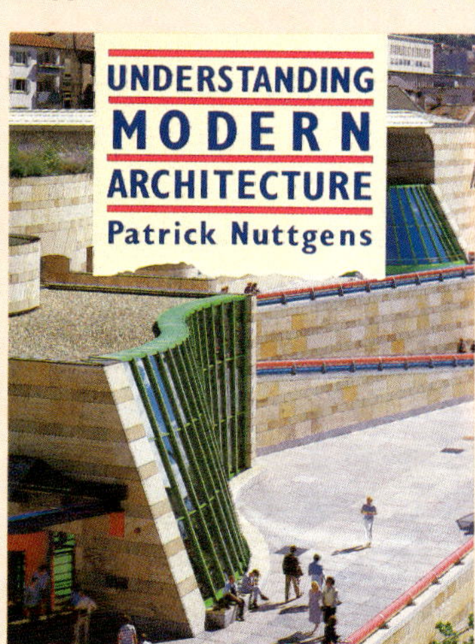

Patrick Nuttgens' introduction to 20th-century architecture paying particular emphasis, as might be expected, on Lutyens as hero and progressing to the 'Anonymity of the International Style' and beyond. Extended picture captions by Bridget Nuttgens provide useful summaries of many of the most influential buildings around the world.

The Decorative Twenties and The Decorative Thirties
both by Martin Battersby, revised Philippe Garner
Herbert Press, London, 1988
224pp, b&w and colills, cloth, £19.95
Art Deco Source Book
Patricia Bayer
Phaidon, Oxford, 1988
192 pp, col ills. cloth £19.95

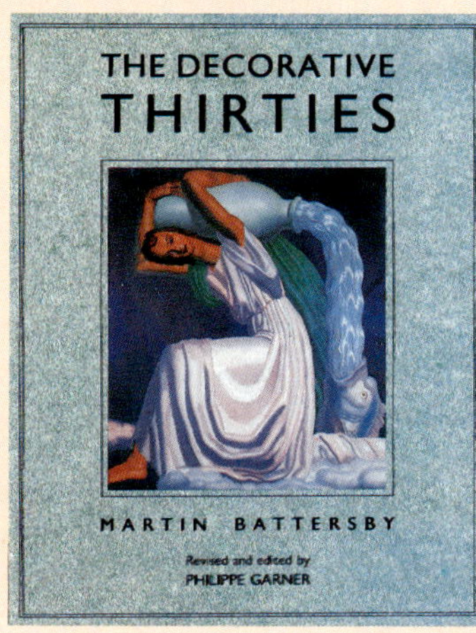

Martin Battersby's books on the 20s and 30s originally published in 1969 and 71 respectively are impressive scholarly and readable studies of the decorative arts in these two decades of exceptional importance for design. The first book begins with a study of France where so much of the work was

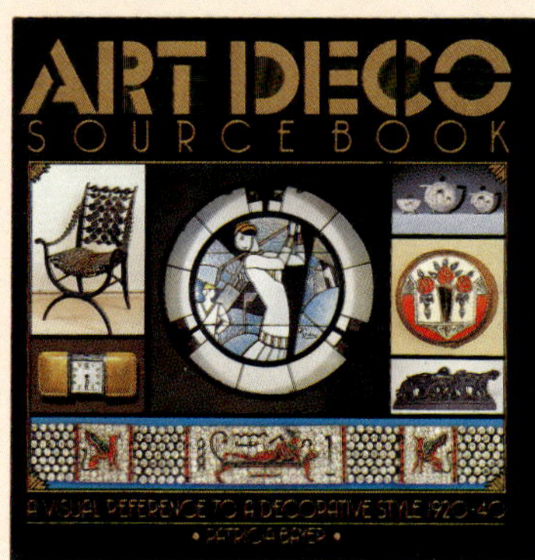

centred and where the important 1925 Exhibition of Decorative Arts was held and then moves on to look at England and America. *The Decorative Thirties* deals with the whole international spectrum, both·cover the wide areas of design and profile individually several of the most important designers such as Rex Whistler, Schiaparelli and Pavel Tchelitchew. Patricia Bayer's book is attractively produced in square format with good colour reproductions, it picks a rather smaller number of chief examples from each area with helpful descriptive captions. It provides a useful introductory pictorial survey, maybe more aimed at interior decorators influenced by such styles today than at an historical understanding of the design principles involved, for such and for its use of contemporary sources and archive photographs, the reissue of the Battersby books is welcome.

Norman Foster
Aldo Benedetti
Zanichelli, Bologna, 1988
206pp, b&w ills, paper, lire 15,000

The latest in Zanichelli's *serie di architettura* is a monograph on Norman Foster as prime exponent of High-Tech. With projects from early Team 4 days in 1963 to recent work in 1985 it presents a useful survey although unfortunately is let down by poor-quality reproductions.

The Mind and Art of Giovanni Battista Piranesi
John Wilton-Ely
Thames & Hudson, London, 1988
304pp, 391 b&w ills, paper, £18.95

The first paperback edition of this work. As well as full-page reproductions of the complete *Vedute di Roma*

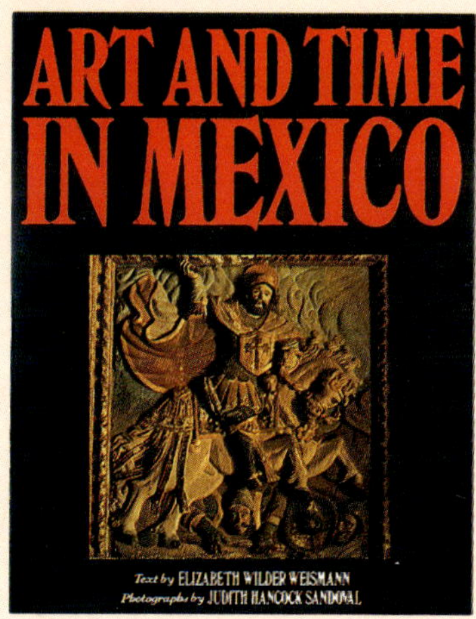

(revealed in part as a determination to prove the genius of Roman architecture with its Etruscan heritage over that of the Greek espoused by Laugier) and the *Carceri d'Invenzione*, the text by John Wilton-Ely covers Piranesi's life and ideas his archaeological researches, his little-known interior designs and his subsequent influence on Neo-Classical architecture: 'It was Piranesi's *Carceri* that taught Dance's generation the expressive potential of design based on the highly original handling of Classical forms amplified by exaggeration in scale and texture.' The fantasy-horror world of the *Carceri* is related both to Tiepolo's *capricci* and the emotional milieu of Burke's *Enquiry into the Sublime and Beautiful*, with their complex visions achieved through graphic mastery of tone and scale.

Art and Time in Mexico
Elizabeth Weismann, photographs by Judith Hancock Sandoval
Harper & Row, London, 1988
284pp, b&w ills, some col, paper, £13.95

Mexican colonial architecture and sculpture in all its Baroque vibrancy and flourishing vulgarity. Above all, lively narrative church facades with figures in deep relief, in the meeting of Spanish colonialism and Mexican life.

Environmental Aesthetics
Edited by Jack L Nasar
CUP, Cambridge, 1988
529 pp, b&w ills, cloth, £45

Collection of short academic papers on the philosophy, psychology and design applications of aesthetics in architecture, landscape and urban planning. The relationship between physical stimuli and human perception as a means to understanding how man is affected by his environment and ways in which it could be improved.

Portuguese Design

jects (furniture, lighting, vases, carpets) encompass a range of individual styles but seem to share a liking for simple geometric forms and an interesting range of exotic woods and metal finishes.

The *Rawhajpoutalahs* extendible table in aluminium and sucupira wood, designed by Pedro Silva Dias, is part of a new venture by Lisbon-based company Loja da Atalaia, which aims to promote furniture and objects designed by a group of young Portuguese architects and designers. Produced in high-quality limited editions the ob-

Lighting Design

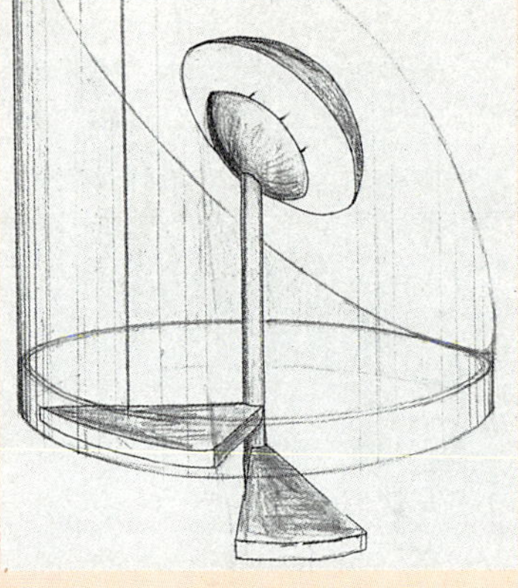

'I design both sculpturally and atmospherically with light . . . I use qualities present in natural light like the colour of the light or climatic effcts as well as artificial light to simultaneously create an atmosphere of drama and tranquility.' That lighting can transform the emotional and atmospheric effectof an environment lies behind the work of London-based Italian lighting designer Umberto di Zenzo. Exploiting the

new technological developments that have produced an unprecedented range of light sources, Di Zenzo aims to maximise the sculptural and effects of light in creating mood and if necessary where the products in the market place are too functionalist will design new lighting concepts or lighting systems to suit specific applications. His clients have included private individuals and multi-national corporations and commissions from small flats to large offices.

Ipswich Docks

With docklands all over the British Isles undergoing regeneration, Norwich architects Feilden and Mawson have successfully combined modern glass technology with the retension of historic elements in their refurbishment of the Home Warehouse a redundant granary in the Ipswich docks. Using Solascrene Silver sealed glass, an advanced reflective solar control

THE ART SHOP

AT THE ROYAL COLLEGE OF ART

BOOKS • MAGAZINES • ARTISTS' MATERIALS

POST-MODERN OBJECTS
INCLUDING COFFEE POTS, KETTLES, DISHES AND PLATES BY
ALDO ROSSI, MICHAEL GRAVES, ETTORE SOTTSASS
RICHARD SAPPER AND ROBERT VENTURI
(see Art & Design 3-4/87)

MEMPHIS JEWELLERY BY ETTORE SOTTSASS AND ROBERT STERN
ORIGINAL WORKS BY RCA STUDENTS

KENSINGTON GORE, LONDON SW7 ℅ 01-589 1790 Entrance opposite the Royal Albert Hall. Open Monday–Saturday 10.00–6.00 and all views.

glass, the focal point of the building is the series of glazed arches at the front. Inside, some of the original machinery was retained so as to keep the building's industrial and maritime character and maintain historical continuity, appropriate for this UK headquarters of a European container shipping line.

Building the Biennale

At the same time as the Palazzo Ducale is the venue for an exhibition of projects by 12 Italian architects for the restoration of the Italian Pavilion of

the Venice Biennale, the Architectural Department of the Biennale of Venice has also announced an international competition for restoration of the Palazzo del Cinema at the Lido of Venice. A number of architects have already been invited to participate but the competition is open to all architects. Further information is available from the Paolo Scibelli/Paolo Cimarosti, Architectural Department of the Biennale of Venice, tel 041-5226514.

Barratts in Brighton

Development of Brighton Marina continues with the release of Barratt's luxury waterside homes. Making use of mooring facilities and water views, the range of houses and apartments are traditionally designed to reflect Brighton's Regency heritage, through such elements as bow fronts and balconies. Internally fittings are luxurious, and on the corner houses spacious

floor plans are unconventional to fit the marina site.

Dutch Architectural Institute

A competition to design a building for the new Dutch Architectural Institute in the Museum park in Rotterdam resulted in an exhibition in July and

August at the Boymans-van Beuningen Museum of the proposals of six architectural practices – Jo Coenen, Jan Benthem/Mels Crouwel, Hubert-Jan Henket, Rem Koolhaas/OMA, Wim Quist and Luigi Snozzi. The brief asked for facilities for a variety of activities including exhibitions, receptions, study rooms and archive facilities as well as restaurants for the public for the Institute which should open in 1992.

Leaning Tower of Pizza

The world's largest pizza delivery company has unveiled plans for a new office tower to be built near their headquarters at Ann Arbor, Michigan. President of Domino's Pizzas, Thomas S Monaghan, is an enthusiastic patron of architecture in the USA whose other projects include a Frank Lloyd Wright museum, the reconstruction of a Frank Lloyd Wright Utzonian house and the Domino's Pizzas list of 'The World's Top 30 Architects' – some of whom they hope will build luxury homes at 'The Settlement' nearby. However, this tower designed by Gunnar Birketts and Associates is far from Lloyd Wright, a 30-storey, glass-clad structure which cantilevers 15 degrees.

Indispensable Tools

For clients, the architectural model is frequently the most easily comprehensible design format, as well as often being a beautiful object in its own right. Nearly 100 models for a wide range of projects were on show recently at the biennial Salon of the Association of Consultant Architects at the Royal Academy of Arts in London.

STRADA NOVISSIMA, VENICE BIENNALE, 1982

THE ARCHITECTURE OF PLURALISM
John Melvin

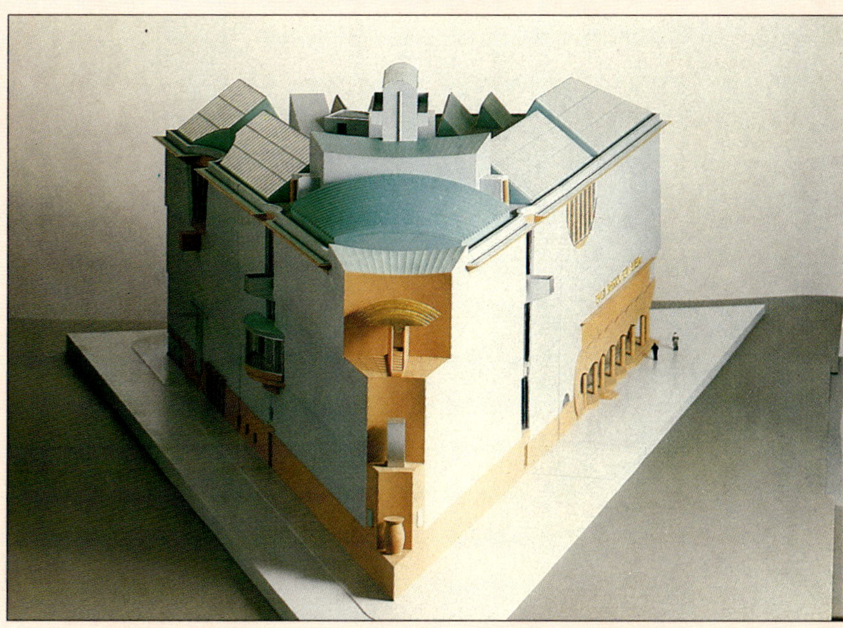

HANS HOLLEIN, FRANKFURT MUSEUM OF MODERN ART, VIEW OF MODEL

The fourth symposium of the Academy Forum on October 3rd was organised to coincide with the celebrations of the 21st anniversary of the founding of the Academy Group by Andreas Papadakis. It brought together the elements which had provided the themes for the earlier symposia in the series: Post-Modernism, Deconstruction, The New Classicism – all combine to make the current architectural scene richly pluralistic and more exciting

than it has been for decades. Given the broad scope of the debate, it was appropriate that this was also the first symposium to be held outside London: the venue was Frankfurt, at the invitation of the Director of the German Architectural Museum, Heinrich Klotz.

The subject of the symposium was pluralism and the new-found freedom of direction in architecture. We are all pluralists now; even Gorbachov, head of the most centrally controlled state, now embraces pluralism in the form of *perestroika* and *glastnost*. In the industrialised West, where political pluralism has generally prevailed for 200 years, the issue is taking on a greater urgency as consumerism assumes a near-transcendental character. Underlying this is the recognition that pluralism, almost by definition, is social in character and has to do with our moral life, the human condition and how we view the world: we are pluralistic in so far as we exist side by side with others.

An underlying backbone for the theme was provided by an article specially written for the symposium by Christian Norberg-Schulz, who asked how one might answer the question prompted by Deconstruction: 'is it possible and meaningful to create order out of the desperate confusion of our time . . .?' He suggested that the solution and the justification for the wealth of variety today might be found in the lessons of American architecture, a return to the real world and to *genius loci*: 'does not the idea of distinct islands of meaning contradict my definition of the pluralist world as a togetherness of interacting cultures? Not necessarily. The islands may not interact spatially, but since they are based on a common, basic language of architectural forms,

mutual understanding and respect becomes possible . . . diversity does not mean arbitrary invention, but rather different expressions within a common language.'

Any new architecture has to recognise this new pluralist world, just as it has to repudiate the monotheism of the International Style. This was illustrated by Robert Stern, who welcomed the idea of pluralism without necessarily defining it, except in terms of his own buildings, these being largely houses in the American tradition for rich clients. For Stern there could be no scientific brief nor could there be any mechanistic solution to an architectural problem, which was for him to do with finding the right form to sustain and re-vivify the institution that is particularly well defined by the American house. One of his early projects was the Wiseman House, Montauk, built in the 60s, which appeared to push the forms of Venturi to an extreme. Stern now rejects this clamour for novelty, pointing out that in domestic architecture there are very good reasons for conventional forms, which have evolved over time and are still pregnant with meaning. It has also to be remembered that Modernism came late to America and most Americans do not live happily with its negative strictures and rejection of past forms. For Europeans architecture is associated with the City and this is often Classical: for the 19th-century American the City was as often as not regarded as a mere corrupt necessity. Classicism nevertheless found its place and was incorporated into the individual suburban house, the quintessential American expression of Classicism being, in Stern's view, the well-known Low House at Bristol, Rhode Island, by McKim Meade & White with its

Bruno Minardi via Traversari n.6 Ravenna

BRUNO MINARDI AND ELISABETTA MARRAF

simple, wide gable forming a low-slung temple-like front. This form was to be found everywhere as a vernacular expression of an American ideal. Stern himself has taken this and repeated it, for example, at Farm Neck, Oak Buffs, Massachusetts. The challenge for the early American architect was to tame the wilderness, therefore the American house tended to embrace the landscape and frame its views. These forms still have meaning even if the wilderness today may be one of urban blight or the parking lot – not solely an American experience. A recent project of Stern's has been to restore a 20-year-old extension to Jefferson's University of Virginia. The University was perhaps the pre-eminent American example of that marriage between Colonial and European Classicism which has the power through its Classical forms to speak for all Americans, a pluralistic nation if ever there was one. Perhaps the most compelling illustrations that Stern put forward for pluralism were those presented by the pluralism within Classical architecture itself. He reminded us that even at the height of the American Civil War work could still proceed on the dome of the Capitol and that Lutyens' New Delhi, after the expulsion of the English, could be taken over by the Indians without any difficulty, whereas Le Corbusier's Chandirgarh, undeniably a great piece of Modern architecture, has

never been accepted indigenously.

Hans Hollein, coming from a different tradition, was able to put forward an alternative interpretation of pluralism, and we were treated to a virtuoso display of synergics. Two of his most recent works are the large mixed development of offices and shops near St Stephen's Cathedral in Vienna and his Art Gallery nearing completion in Frankfurt. Much of the quality and pleasure of these buildings reside in their planning, with the space in both buildings being manipulated with an almost tangible sensuousness. Externally Hollein is unashamedly eclectic. One facade could incorporate dissimulated elements unacknowledged in another facade. All this is carried out with the brilliance and sleight-of-hand of a juggler. The extraneous and the disparate were all brought together with that sense of style which Hollein has been able to display from the very first in his two small shops in Vienna. Hollein seems to be able to draw on that specific Viennese tradition of shopfitting design where multiple scale and patterns finally come together and are resolved in a satisfying unity, a legacy perhaps of the Secessionists.

Rob Krier, on the other hand, had little time for categories or definitions. His concern was with mending and repairing the fragmented City that has suffered under the misguided hand of

VILLE CONTEMPORAINE, WATERCOLOUR

modern redevelopment. We were treated to a now-familiar tour of major European cities which have received his recipes and proposals for their repair. His approach was to return to a traditional syntax of spaces and forms which were readily understood and recognised. Out of this philosophy there appeared to be emerging a reassuring portfolio of work of real urban excellence and maturity.

Günther Behnisch treated us to what amounted to a catalogue raisonnée of his life's work, with a commnetary that had all the ambiguity of the Delphic oracle. It was interesting to see how an architect working in the Scharoun mould of German Expressionism can change and tailor his response over a period of time. It says a great deal about the liveliness of present German architecture as it does about the courage and industrial vitality of German patronage.

Charles Jencks welcomed the idea of pluralism and claimed that it was worth fighting for, however hard this might be in practice. The term had to be defined; the architecture of pluralism had also to include those architects who had adopted various theories of chaos. However he saw that there were various degrees of chaos: there was organised chaos and disorganised chaos and a full spectrum between the two. Eisenman, Tschumi,

Koolhaas and Gehry all applied various chaos theories. If these appear somewhat epistemologically, it may be the Japanese such as Hiroshi Hara and Kazuo Shinohara, who also espouse chaos theories, whom we may really find difficult to relate to as their culture of the city is so different from the Western experience.

While he had talked up to then about architects working on the edge of critical theory, Jencks said he felt all architects could, to use Sir Isiah Berlin's well-known definition, be divided into either hedgehogs or foxes or – to use his own updated version of the simile – octopuses or whales. The fox or the octopus, we were reminded, knows many things, but the hedgehog or whale knows one big thing. This division remains a psychological constant and tends to separate those who relate everything to a single central vision or unifying principle from others who see all as chaos or accident and who pursue many ends, often unrelated. Dante was a hedgehog, while Shakespeare was a fox. Alberti, on the other hand, according to Jencks, was a fox but Palladio a hedgehog.

It was his contention that the problem with modern architects is that there is a tendency for foxes to become hedgehogs and, as in nature, so we were assured, hedgehogs eventually eat each other, 'the whale … the kind of Maoist beast that would

JOHN MELVIN & PARTNERS, 1-6 MERCERS PLACE, BROOK GREEN, LONDON

swallow other fish into its grand historical synthesis; while as a substitute for the fox we can proffer the octopus, because with its many arms and protrusions, it is much more visibly a pluralist.' This cannibalism found its obvious parallel in the reality of consumerism, where objects and styles are quickly subsumed within a marketable product and immediately become devalued. This has an effect on the use of language within any system, as language essentially depends on a set of opposites to give the sign its meaning. The lifespan of any movement now appears to be about two years before it becomes bankrupted by over-exposure and devalued by consumption – by this reckoning Post-Modernism is definitely passé. At this stage Jencks introduced the star of the show, which was neither a speaker nor a theory but a building, the recently completed Landeszentralbank in Frankfurt. By comparison with Foster's Hongkong Bank, this remarkable building has received little press, perhaps because it has taken its place so effortlessly in the banking quarter of Frankfurt. Nonetheless, it must surely come to be regarded not only as a landmark for the architecture of pluralism but as one of the great buildings of the decade. Its gradual and selective exposure to the media can therefore only be welcomed.

What the two sessions clearly showed was the social character of pluralism. From the time when man emerged from the primordial swamp he had to develop institutions to cope with his individual needs and capacities and to do this he had to form the collectives or communities which we now call society. Indeed it was one of the functions of architecture to give form to these institutions. Many of our greatest myths and sagas from the Tower of Babel onwards have been about precisely how we recognise, understand, use and improve these forms and orders amidst the seeming chaos that surrounds us. Running as a continuous thread through this endeavour is always the impulse towards an ideal or utopia. At times, especially after some crisis, there is a temptation to seek a single-perspective vision of perfection, to build a Tower of Babel, with of course the ensuing consequences.

This was the error of Gropius who claimed that the principles behind the design of a chair and a town plan were the same, a dangerously false assumption. It was this single-point perspective that became the lot of the Modern Movement, in particular the International Style, colouring much of the first part of this troubled century. Yet reality or meaning can never be found through a single vision but rather resides in the confusion of its kaleidoscopic pieces. It is precisely these pieces which we are

BEHNISCH & PARTNER, UNIVERSITY LIBRARY, EICHSTÄTT

now beginning to study. Deconstruction, Post-Modernism, the New Classicism – all naturally fall within the compass of pluralism. Recognising this injects something new into the framework of Modernism, in that an architect such as Robert Stern can now produce original architecture which acknowledges and plays upon an existing tradition. This is the fundamental difference between today's architecture and that of the International Style.

The symposium was concluded by the opening of an exhibition on the theme of pluralism showing the work of 21 canonic architects selected by Andreas Papadakis. The architects included Leon and Rob Krier, Norman Foster, Richard Meier, Robert Venturi, Michael Graves, Frank Gehry, Terry Farrell, Bernard Tschumi, OMA and Aldo Rossi. Pluralism is also the subject of a major book, *The Architecture of Pluralism*, to be published in 1989, a summation of the thought-provoking articles and seminal projects from 21 years of *Architectural Design*.

An interesting aspect of the exhibition is that all the architects are represented by actual buildings rather than mere paper projects – ten years ago this would probably not have been the case. It is perhaps a testament to museums such as the German Architecture Museum and publications such as *Architectural Design* that ideas in the form of drawings can now infuse so swiftly into the body of architectural practice to produce buildings of such interest and distinction. It should be remembered that drawings are different from buildings and it is precisely because we experience and therefore understand the two differently that drawings and their associated images are so important. This has been true throughout the history of architecture. Lord Burlington did not after all replicate Palladio, even though he had Palladio's drawings. And English Georgian is markedly different from that of Colonial America, even though they may have come from the same copybooks. The great advantage of drawings is that they can be interpreted (or misinterpreted) to suit our particular needs and thus they become an important instrument in the regional and national variety which we may call pluralism. This impulse and necessity for variety and our inability to ever fully describe it or pin it down was perhaps best summed up by the Frankfurt School philosopher Wittgenstein, in his dictum that we should not look for meaning in any hard or fast sense of that word but rather look for meaning in use which in turn will be determined by forms of life. This is what the recognition of pluralism permits us to do.

ADRIAN BERG, *GLOUCESTER GATE, REGENT'S PARK*, 1982, OIL

URBAN CONCEPTS
Architectural Design Vol 58 No 11/12-1988

Known for her ideas of community involvement, this issue looks at Denise Scott Brown's approach to American urban planning, focusing in particular on her urban plan for Memphis, an in-depth scheme covering all aspects of planning, aesthetics, politics and community participation. There are two major essays by Denise Scott Brown: 'Between Three Stools', a personal view of urban-design education, and 'The Public Realm'. The issue also includes an illuminating discussion between Denise Scott Brown and architectural critics Simon Jenkins and Martin Pawley held recently at the Tate Gallery as well as an essay placing Scott Brown in an international context and comparing her ideas to those in Britain.

THE NEW ROMANTICS
Art & Design Vol 4 No 9/10-1988

This issue examines new romantic artists in their international context. A powerful component in the recent resurgence of representational art has been the unleashing of the fantastical, the surreal and the visionary together with a landscape art that draws on the scenery, forms and spiritual qualities of the natural world. An extensive interview with Robert Rosenblum and essays by Keith Patrick, Malcolm Yorke, John Griffiths, Giles Auty, Michael Greenhalgh and Mary Rose Beaumont attempt to identify and define the new trend of romanticism, its relationship to art history, its legacy both in Britain and internationally, the qualities that make it an art of today and the different directions it is taking.

Individual issues £7.95/US$14.95 + £1/US$2 p&p

SUBSCRIPTION FORM

☐ I wish to subscribe to **Architectural Design** at the full rate
☐ I wish to subscribe to **AD** at the student rate

☐ I wish to subscribe to **Art & Design** at the full rate
☐ I wish to subscribe to **A&D** at the student rate

☐ I wish to subscribe to **AD** and **A&D** at the full rate
☐ I wish to subscribe to **AD** and **A&D** at the student rate

☐ Starting date: Issue No.................................Year ....

☐ **Payment enclosed by Cheque/ P.O./ Draft.** Value £ / US$ ....
☐ **Please charge** £..**to my credit card**

Expiry date: ....

Account No:

☐ American Express ☐ Access/ Mastercharge/ Eurocard
☐ Diners Club ☐ Barclaycard/ Visa

SUBSCRIPTION RATES

	UK	EUROPE	OVERSEAS
ARCHITECTURAL DESIGN			
Full rate	£45.00	£55.00	US$99.50
Student rate	£39.50	£49.50	US$89.50
ART & DESIGN			
Full rate	£35.00	£39.50	US$75.00
Student rate	£29.00	£35.00	US$45.00
ARCHITECTURAL DESIGN AND ART & DESIGN			
Full combined rate	£65.00	£75.00	US$135.00
Student combined rate	£59.50	£69.50	US$120.00

Signature...
Name...
Address...
....
....

Please send this form with your payment/ credit card authority direct to:

ACADEMY GROUP LTD 7/8 HOLLAND ST, LONDON W8 4NA ✆ 01-402-2141

Imitation & Innovation

HAMMOND, BEEBY & BABKA, HOLE-IN-THE-WALL GANG CAMP, DINING HALL

ROBERT ADAM, DOGMERSFIELD PARK PROJECT

An Architectural Design Profile

Imitation & Innovation

ROBERT STERN, OBSERVATORY HILL DINING HALL, UNIVERSITY OF VIRGINIA

ACADEMY EDITIONS · LONDON/ST MARTIN'S PRESS · NEW YORK

Acknowledgements

Front Cover: Cenicacelaya and Saloña, Rural Centre, La Rigada, Muskiz; *Back Cover:* Leon Krier, Seaside Tower, Florida; *Inside Front Cover:* Allan Greenberg, Four Variations on the Whorl, US Department of State, Washington, photo by Richard Cheek; *Inside Back Cover:* Drawings by second-year students of the Madrid School of Architecture, *clockwise from left:* P Pajares Ayuela, J Rodríguez Henche, N Barragan Lara, M L Carrilero G del Villar, L C Hernandez Cano, A Gallego, courtesy of Helena Iglesias; *Prelim pages:* Hammond, Beeby and Babka, Hole-in-the-Wall Gang Camp; Robert Adam, Dogmersfield Park Project; Robert Stern, Observatory Hill Dining Hall, photo by T Whitney Cox; Iñiguez and Ustarroz, New Faculty Building, University of the Basque Country.

We should like to thank Lucien Steil for his work and enthusiasm in guest-editing this issue. We are also grateful to all the architects concerned for their help in providing drawings and photographs of their projects. In addition we should like to thank the following:

Quatremère de Quincy
6-7: The photograph on page 6 is by Dominique Delauney.

Robert Stern
20-27: Raymond Gastil and Joanne Lehrfeld of Robert Stern architects for providing transparencies. T Whitney Cox for his photographs of Observatory Hill Dining Hall, University of Virginia, and Marblehead House.

Quinlan Terry
32-7: Mr Thody of Haslemere Estates and Chris Parkinson of Richard Ellis for all their help in providing recent photographs and information on Richmond Riverside.

Allan Greenberg
38-49: Allan Greenberg for providing photographs of the Department of State on page 38 by Richard Cheek and of the farmhouse in Connecticut by Peter Mauss/Esto.

Leon Krier
50-59: Bernard Neis for his commentary on the Luxembourg scheme.

John Simpson
78-80: Carl Laubin for providing a transparency of his painting.

Editor: Dr Andreas C Papadakis

First published in Great Britain in 1988 by *Architectural Design*
an imprint of the
ACADEMY GROUP LTD, 7 HOLLAND STREET, LONDON W8 4NA
ISBN: 0-85670-954-9 (UK)

Architectural Design Profile 75 is published as part of *Architectural Design* Vol 58 9/10-1988
Published in the United States of America by
ST MARTIN'S PRESS, 175 FIFTH AVENUE, NEW YORK 10010

Printed and bound in Singapore

Contents

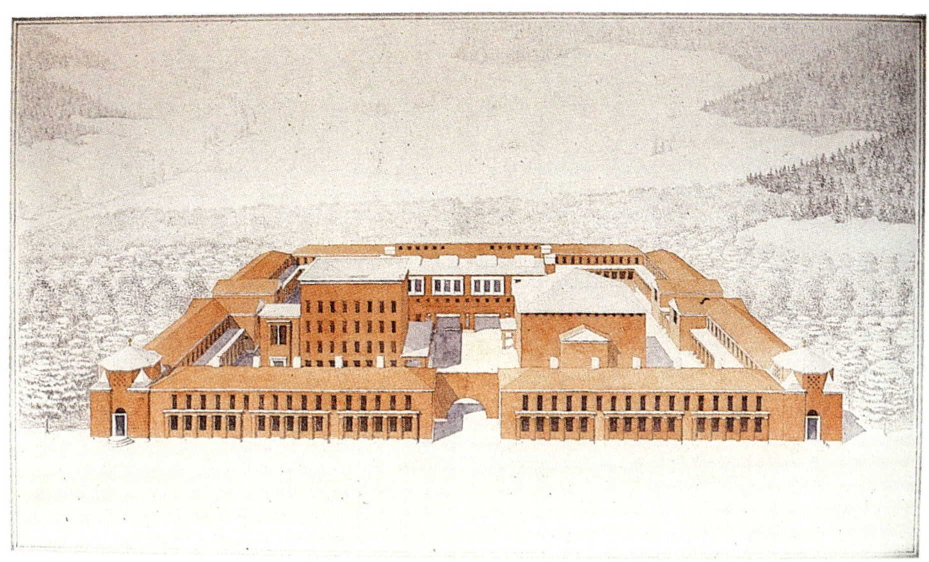

INIGUEZ & USTARROZ, PROJECT FOR A NEW PHILOSOPHY FACULTY AT THE BASQUE UNIVERSITY

THE STAIRCASE OF THE BIBLIOTHEQUE MAZARINE IN PARIS, A FAVOURITE HAUNT OF QUATREMERE DE QUINCY'S

QUATREMÈRE DE QUINCY
On Imitation

IMITATION: Each art has, in nature, both a general model and a model that is specific to it.

Here the word 'nature' should be understood in the broadest sense to mean the domain of physical beings and the rule of moral or intellectual things. Since all the arts have a common model in nature . . . it follows that they also have rules of imitation in common. Thus we can speak of a universal grammar which comprises the rules of language, inasmuch as language, an attribute exclusive to man, is founded on a number of principles deriving from the laws of intelligence and feelings, with a grammar specific to each language or idiom which comprises the local variations and particular modifications made by each country to the art of indicating thoughts with sounds or signs.

For an art to be called an art of *imitation*, it is not necessary that its model be based in an obvious, perceptible manner on physical and material nature. This kind of model is accorded only to the two arts which address themselves to the eye through the imitation of bodies and colours. Nor is it necessary for all the arts in the domain of poetry to be based on a model as easy to grasp or conceive as that of the dramatic arts, which finds ready portraits for copying in the characters, passions and absurdities of society. The other kinds of poetry, though they do not have such clearly defined models, benefit no less from the privilege of imitation: only the nature which they imitate, or which is the special point of view of these arts, has something more abstract, more general, requiring a broader view. To see the kind of *imitation* which concerns the poet in a limited way: to restrain him to what one would call *imitative poetry*, to onomatopoeias, or to a choice of expressions and sounds pertaining to resemble the thing that they signify, seems tantamount to counterfeiting its appearance.

So when you hear that nature is the model of all the fine arts, you have to keep in mind that the idea of nature should not be limited to that which is perceptible, material, or which falls under the rule of the senses. Nature exists as much in that which is invisible as in those things which scize the eye. Thus taking nature as one's model means imitating it by adhering to the same rules, in certain works of arts, which nature herself follows: it means scrutinising the intentions underlying the form of living beings, the principles to which nature subordinates her action, the direction that she gives to her means, the aim or the end towards which she is moving. Imitating does not necessarily mean making the likeness of a thing, because one cannot imitate the work and imitate the worker. One therefore imitates nature by doing not *what* she does, but *as* she does: that is to say, one can still imitate her action when one cannot imitate her work.

The imitation which is truly distinctive of architecture and the architect – which associates one and the other with the glory of the fine arts – is based on nature, but considered within the general laws of order and harmony, in the reasons which explain all works, in the principles determining her action. Thus the architect imitates nature when, in the creations dependent on his art, he has followed and made evident the system which nature has developed in all her works.

From Quatremère's Encyclopédie Méthodique de Panckoucke

LUCIEN STEIL
On Imitation

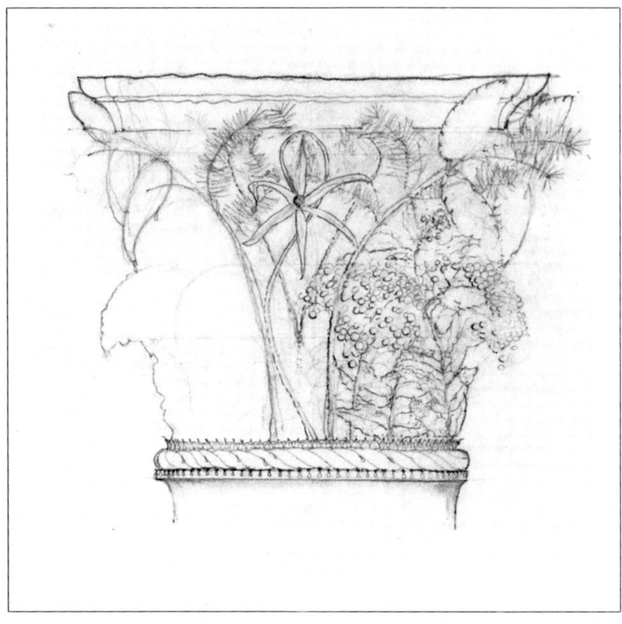

JOHN CZARNECKI, CORINTHIAN CAPITAL

It is difficult to add anything substantial to Quatremere de Quincy's essay *On Imitation* (1823) and *Dictionnaire*, for Quatremère excels in precision and comprehensiveness as well as in depth. His genius proves to be universal. Let me therefore make a case for a conscientious study of his original writings and encourage genuinely original architects and artists to learn from authentic sources. Abandon yourselves, dear readers, to the '*plaisir du*

texte'. Vitruvius' *Ten Books of Architecture*, Palladio's *Four Books of Architecture*, the Abbé Laugier's An *Essay on Architecture*, Alberti's *Ten Books of Architecture*, Quatremère de Quincy's *On Imitation*, Ruskin's *The Seven Lamps of Architecture*, Tessenow's *Handwerk und Kleinstadt*, Schumacher's *Der Geist der Baukunst*, Karl Gruber's *Die Gestalt der Deutschen Stadt* – these are all works of great beauty, in ideas and concepts as well as in genius of writing, expression, composition and style.

The first principle of imitation would thus be to study the originals – to study them radically as first works and to consider them as if nothing had come before them and nothing was to come after. Nothing is more invigorating and refreshing in times of confusion than to go back to origins. Learning and knowing is always a quest for original knowledge: 'The first step we have to make is to examine, if we are allowed the term, the genealogy and relation of our ideas, the causes that have given rise to them, and the characteristics that distinguish them: in a word, to return to the origin and generation of our knowledge.' (d'Alembert, *Discours préliminaire* to the *Encyclopédie*)

Origin and originals

'Architecture (Arche-tectonike) means literally "Form of Origin". If this definition is relevant for the architecture of any organism and structure, it is fundamental for Architecture as the Art of Building. It is not that the principles of Architecture reach into an immemorial past, that but their origin is forever present.' (Leon Krier, *Architectural Design*, 'Houses, Palaces, Cities')

'Origin here means that from and by which something is what it is and as it is. What something is, as it is, we call its essence or nature. The origin of something is the source of its nature.' (Heidegger, *Poetry, Language, Thought*)

The reconstruction of architecture is not concerned with 'pastiches' of any kind but with the rehabilitation of originality. Amidst the debate on the aesthetics of fragments and the 'poetics' of conceptual and constructional inconsistency and confusion, there are imperative reasons for reclaiming the Classical ideals of integrity, harmony, beauty and reason, for questioning the reality of modern architectural production and ideology and re-establishing the legitimacy of architecture as an artistic and intellectual discipline. This means celebrating originality as a nostalgia for origin rather than opting for the euphoria of amnesia. Origin refers of course to historical and geographical as well as mythological and cultural realities but in a truly generative way.

The true forms of origin are reconstructed by a process of imitation as *originals*. By its constant reflection of origin, imitation becomes the legitimate source of originality. Establishing a creative dialogue between 'origin' and 'originals' it allows for invention of permanence and permanence of invention. In a context of continuity, originals themselves become legitimate objects of imitation. They represent the immense patrimony of architecture, the most genial and original inventions of mankind accumulated through millenia of imitation. This nature of imitations is the 'reality' of architecture.

However one crucial question remains unanswered: if imitation is the very issue of architectural invention, and if origin is the very object of imitation, what then is this origin? Many treatises have investigated these beginnings and constructed a theory of origin. A comparative reading of the classic authors like Vitruvius, Alberti, Laugier and Quatremère de Quincy is highly recommended in this context, but it is also fascinating to consult minor authors and historians to study the history of 'beginnings' and so search, in Rykwert's words, for 'the memory of something which cannot but be lost' (In *On Adam's House in Paradise*). Let me make some comments on this question, basing most of my reflections on the authority of the ancient authors. Architecture is without a model in nature. There is no 'natural house' or 'natural city'. The invention of architecture is not an instinctive reaction to being in the world. Architecture is not a survival issue. In the beginning man found shelter in places which nature offered him graciously. Later these different places were synthesised in the invention of architecture. Forms, spaces, materials and natural laws were all assimilated in this immediate confrontation with nature. Nature is thus at the beginning of architecture. Sky, sun and stars, elements, geology, the flora and fauna, elaborate structures and complex shapes, and last but not least, all those natural shelters which existed as a part of the natural world long before man appeared: nests, caves, hives, shells . . . All this great complexity, diversity, contrast and plurality in nature has forever stirred man's imagination and emotions, as well as his philosophical and scientific curiosity. Has it also raised the nostalgia of architecture? Man must have tried very early to materialise and symbolise his relationship with nature. Does architecture not finally achieve the reconciliation of man and the universe by consecrating man's home and the homes of his Gods? (cf A Perez-Gomez in *Architecture and the Crisis of Modern Science*).

The imitation of nature

'It is nature itself in its abstract essence which is taken as a model. It is the order of nature which becomes its archetype and genius.' (Quatremère de Quincy)

If origin means the construction of the universe, the building of the world, there will be an original model (not immediately for architecture, but for imitation) for nature.

'Creation means the repetition of the original creation' writes Mircea Eliade in *The Sacred and the Profane*. This 'original creation' is defined as the 'transformation of chaos into cosmos'. To capture the *essence of nature* – the universal principles of cosmic order and harmony – is the objective of imitation. Imitation thus becomes the creative process synthesising universe and nature into temples, houses, palaces, monuments and cities. The invention of architecture through the imitation of nature means then the original and imaginative synthesis of constructive, formal, harmonious, functional and ecological principles inherent in nature. 'This order which in Nature is hidden and implicit, Architecture makes patent to the eye'(Sir Geoffrey Scott, *The Architecture of Humanism*).

The famous 'primitive hut' is but a metaphor for the origin of architecture in nature. It is however the most radical and inspiring way of exploring the nature of architecture, emphasising the mythical character of origin. What we reconstruct with the primitive hut has no memory; it itself becomes the original paradigm for architecture, the poetical evidence of archaic memories. The primitive hut is a mythical, philosophical and artistic reconstruction, an original model which can be imitated and is thus the very nature of architectural invention.

Quatremère de Quincy's discussion of the 'little rustic hut' is elaborate and complex. His model evolves from the 'cabane symbolique', or the primitive timber construction defined as an 'allegorical prototype', through its refinement by 'analogical imitation' of the human body. Architecture finally equals nature and becomes the 'rival of its model'.

The imitation, the copy and the pastiche

This reading might be somewhat confusing to those who don't differentiate between copy, pastiche and imitation. Imitation is a truly inventive and creative process which combines the seriousness of true scholarship, the talent of true art, the intelligence of true inventiveness, the skills of true craftsmanship and the imagination of true creativity. Its objective is to create something 'new' out of the synthesis of an original model. Imitation is the *reconstruction of an original,* whereas a copy is merely a *reproduction of a precedent*. They are thus fundamentally different in intention, artistic and intellectual process and result. Imitation is based on the critical, selective and inventive process of a living tradition, whereas the copy is concerned with the mechanical and literal replication of originals. Imitation addresses both essence and form, where as a copy is interested only in appearance. Imitation is not concerned with similitude or dissimilarity: it has a much more profound understanding of originality, invention and of what architecture is and has always been; its preoccupation is to get to the essence of things.

A pastiche is a partial and imperfect copy, a simplified reproduction of dominant stylistic and compositional elements that lacks however the rigour and discipline of a real copy. Though a copy is interested only in appearance, it is reproduction requiring the seriousness and skill of the craftsman, whereas pastiche is not so much interested in appearance as in the impression of appearance. For the pasticheur anything is good enough to recreate impressions (there are, of course, true and false impressions, good and bad pastiches).

Imitation in architecture deserves more attention in contemporary discussion. Architecture is expressive of civilisation and its condition, at the same time both articulating memory and defining place. Architectural critics have been very quick to condemn authentic traditions but if more critical interest and attention were now given to the study of traditional architecture its superiority in design and building, its modernity in ecological and socio-cultural terms and its success in building a beautiful, comfortable and durable world would soon become clear.

Architecture has to depend on tradition, as appropriated by imitation. Neither *Zeitgeist* nor *genius loci* can be grasped by individuals or groups in specific periods without a historical distance. Too often these poetical concepts are used for narrow historical interpretations and speculations. Any project in any historical period necessarily deals with time and place and expresses its contemporary or modern situation. Both time and place transcend the limitations of the present and address the complexity of history and mythology. Tradition is history with a project, not history as an undifferentiated description of the past. It refers to the intelligence and creativity of past generations, as well as to memory – of the past and of the future. Imitation mediates actively between tradition and reconstruction. It contributes to the constant enrichment of architecture and city building by new originals. It is concerned with the nature of things, their true appearance, and it reestablishes economy, propriety and beauty as the first principles of architecture. Imitation actualises the modernity of tradition in the context of reconstruction in which ecological, economic, humanistic and cultural concerns are intelligently integrated.

———— * ————

LUDWIG HOFFMANN, SQUARE IN ATHENS

JOSÉ IGNACIO LINAZOSORO
The Theory and Practice of Imitation and the Crisis in Classicism

K F SCHINKEL, INTERIOR PERSPECTIVE OF ST GERTRAUD'S CHURCH IN BERLIN

José Ignacio Linazosoro, himself a practising architect, traces the historical evolution of the theory of imitation and shows that the concept does not necessarily preclude models other than the Classical. It is a theory sufficiently rich to accommodate Schinkel's mastery of Berlin's Hanseatic Gothic as well as Classical traditions and, when Classicism was undergoing a crisis with the rise of Modernism, Behrens' attempt at a synthesis between tradition and technology.

From the Renaissance to the beginning of the 19th century, all theoreticians of art and architecture resorted to the concept of mimesis or imitation in order to explain the origin of the arts. The symbolic figuration of the Byzantine period and the Middle Ages was abandoned; art would directly approach Nature in search of its means of expression. The last and most illustrious of these theoreticians was undoubtedly Quatremère de Quincy, who, in his *Dictionnaire* and in his voluminous essay *De l'imitation*, developed a precise argument on the subject.[1] Quatremère established mimesis or imitation as the common starting point for any process of artistic production and also maintained that the principal enjoyment in a work of art lies in comparing the image with the model. Thus imitation 'proves to be fictitious in relation to the reality of the model' and, in its turn, 'the image proves to be incomplete in relation to the imitation'. In fact, to imitate does not for him mean to 'copy' but rather to 'represent' the laws of nature — that is to say, the order and harmony of nature and the model ought thus to be considered as an 'ideal', rather than as being concrete..

For Quatremère imitation is also the basis of 'invention', which simply consists of a new combination of pre-existing elements:

> It is agreed, in effect, that man does not create in the elementary sense of the word, but that he simply finds new combinations of pre-existing elements; the same is true for the inventor who also finds such combinations . . . Thus it can be said that all the arts have, in the field of imitation, inexhaustible resources for satisfying this appetite.[2]

The concepts of model and image also complement each other in the notion of 'type', which can be identified with the class or essence of the artistic work. This differs from the model in that, 'the model, as

understood in the practical execution of art, is an object which must be repeated as it is; the type, on the other hand, is an object from which an infinite number of works can be conceived, bearing no resemblance to each other . . . The word "type" indicates less the picture of an object to be faithfully copied or imitated than the idea of a basic principle which must itself govern the model.'[3]

In architecture these concepts, most particularly imitation, required specific formulation, since if a precise reference to a natural model was always possible in art or sculpture the same was not true for architecture where the model is necessarily artificial. It was not enough to establish a metaphorical or anthropomorphic relationship, as Vitruvius did with regard to architectural orders and their masculine or feminine properties, what was needed above all was a well-defined and autonomous model from which the mimetic relationship could be established.

In the desire for rationalisation and the search for a model, Abbé Laugier, and indeed the majority of 18th-century treatise writers, used to refer to the 'primitive hut', supposedly the original model for all Greek and Classical architecture. The myth of the 'primitive hut' and its link with a ligneous and architraved model was to become the subject of polemic begun by Piranesi, himself, and the Italians, in general, who were determined to defend the primacy of Roman architecture, with its vaults and walls, over Greek architecture with its architraves.[4]

The radical analysis of history intoduced by Laugier's rationalist thought led Quatremère himself, although also a defender of Greek primacy, to establish a well-founded criticism of the Abbé's position:

> Thus, when we recognise an imitation of the hut or of primitive

types of framework in, for example, the Greek architecture, which has become that of all Europe, we should not think that the architect who composes within this architectural system is himself imitating these types or this primitive model; he is only adopting an imitation sanctioned by all sorts of examples, by the approval of the centuries and of all cultivated peoples.[5]

In this way Quatremère found a middle way: the experience of history. It was on this experience of sanctioned models that the imitative principle in architecture would be based. But *malgré lui*, at the same time Quatremère underwent a crisis concerning the very model he proposed to imitate. For, if it is history that legitimises the Greek model, could it not also legitimise other alternative models? Whilst recognising the validity of the principle of imitation, what reason was there to reject all the other architectural models and constructional 'types', Roman or medieval for example?

One and a half centuries earlier, Fréart de Chambray in his *'Parallèle'*, had already remarked on the conventionalism of the different versions of Classical orders, at the same time stating his personal preference for some orders over others. In this way the

model, was questioned, since it could only be justified by a generally acknowledged convention. This is why, from the second half of the 17th century, the concept of *style* was gradually put forward as an alternative to the Classical model, leading to the introduction of other architectural models, in particular those from the Middle Ages.

Romantic Classicism

The architecture of the Enlightenment seemed to reinforce the Classical model anew, although revived in such a way as to establish itself first and foremost as a paradigm of rationality and systemisation. Its consequences were however divergent.

On one side emerged the 'utilitarianism' of Durand, Professor of the new Ecole Polytechnique, whose effectiveness as an educator stemmed from his unwillingness to distinguish between the concept of type and the model. The principle of imitation was substituted by a principle of combination based on the existence of 'elements' and 'parts', authentic 'fragments' of an architectural 'model' which, when combined, will give rise to new buildings adapted to new programmes. Although this is undoubtedly a pedestrian outlook, it is effective in its capacity as a

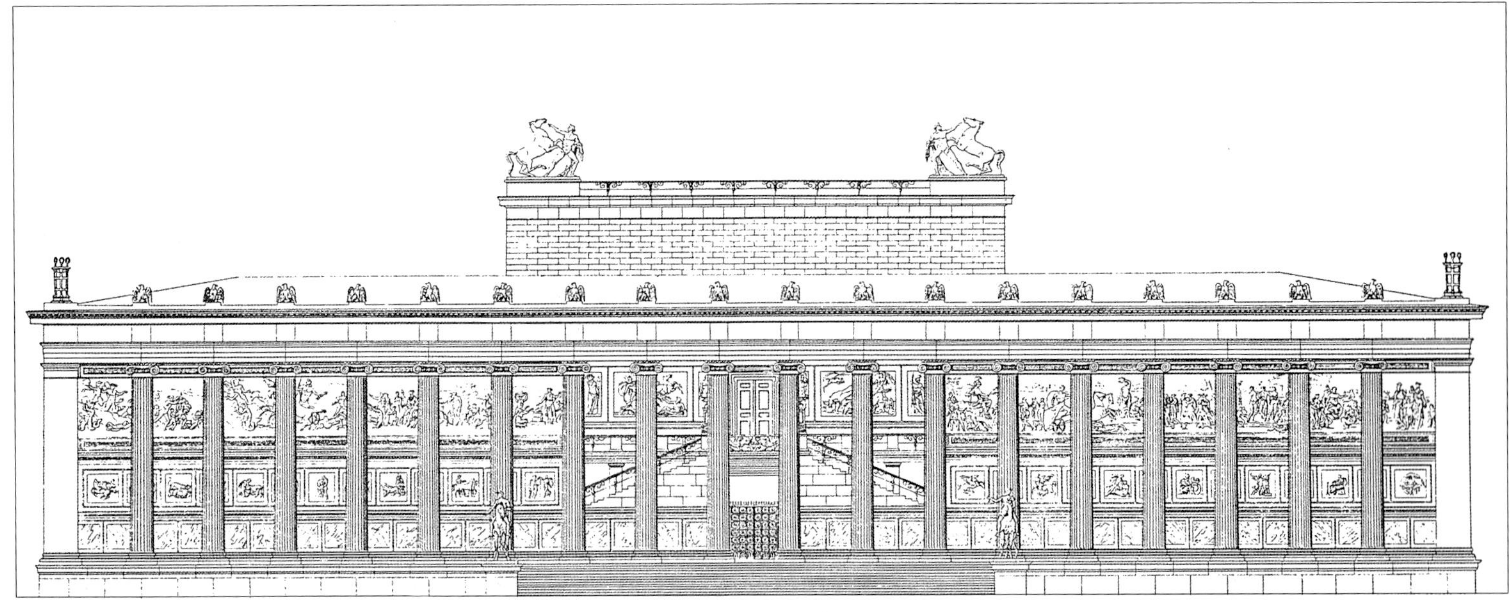

K F SCHINKEL, ALTES MUSEUM, BERLIN

principal protagonists in the *'Querelle'* (Fréart and Perrault with regard to architecture) had introduced the concept of *convention* as a criterion for applying to these orders. Thus Fréart de Chambray affirms: ' . . . I have faithfully transcribed my designs and compared the one with the other, employing such a simple method that you can see in an instant how they all differ; to the point where, by comparing them in this way, everyone has the freedom to choose . . . since they all meet with general approval.'[6]

In short, if at the end of the 18th century the principle of imitation continued to be generally acknowledged, what was still not so well-defined, especially in architecture, was the model to be imitated. It had to be based on acknowledged *conventions*, rather than on an objective reality, and had therefore to be subjected to a criterion of *adaptation* which would justify its practical application. Thus, on the one hand, the reinforcement of the principles of Classical art began to be viewed as an historic constant, founded on the basis of *imitation*. In the case of architecture, this was seen in the constancy of architectural types and, as with the other arts, in the existence of models. On the other hand, the existence of a 'single model' ie, the Classical

project 'manual' which questions the validity of Classical principles, whilst remaining subject to the 'stylistic discipline of Classicism' in its appeal to Classical models.[7] Durand's work, in this sense, was neither 'modern' nor close to the mechanistic and functionalist dictates of the 1820s and 30s, since it stood apart from the 'models' they made use of, where the blurring between type and model is manifest and invention from a model is based no longer on mimesis but on mechanical reproduction. The mechanisms of industrial production would thus be emulated by architects, for architecture began to be seen as an art which was eminently utilitarian, rather than representative or votive. This was not however the only solution to the revolutionary crisis of the end of the 18th century.

In parallel with Durand's utilitarianism, the Beaux-Arts tradition was developed and enriched, not only in France but throughout Europe. Quatremère's *Dictionnaire*, published in 1823, is witness to this. The existence of a unique model to be imitated was now being questioned, although not the principle of imitation or the legacy of history.

The most pressing problem, however, lay in establishing a correlation between model and *adaptation*, bearing in mind the multiplicity of models. In this regard Quatremère, picking up on the theories of Le Camus de Mézières, introduced the concept of *character* as a criterion of selection, although his outlook remained disciplined in comparison with Le Camus' physiognomical tendencies or Ledoux's 'speaking architecture'.[8] Whilst Quatremère was always in favour of the Classical model, his theories also opened the way for the alternative possibilities that would be put into practice by the architects of the period.

For the French theoretician, the foundations of character originate in various aspects of the design. First, 'utility', which can be understood as collective convention. Secondly, the actual composition of the building, ie the ground plan and elevation together with the materials and constructional systems used for building. Finally, the ornamentation or decoration. Throughout the first half of the century, these concepts seem to have been translated into the more or less conventional application of architectural systems to determine specific types of building, beginning the stylistic eclecticism characteristic of the 1880s. An eclecticism which had however different derivations, some more superficial than others.

The first architect to subscribe to this tendency was without synthesis. Both Classical and Gothic models can be recognised in the Bauakademie, an exemplary synthesis which served as a precedent for the best architecture representative of the 19th century. In this way, Schinkel was not only able to revive the 'material' value of brick in medieval Hanseatic architecture and the 'linearity', complexity and gracefulness of Gothic windows, dispensing with all reference to the Classical orders, but also, by the sheer volume or the mighty cornice, to evoke the more permanent values of the Classical model. This is proof of the effectiveness of an 'invention' which consisted, to quote Quatremère, 'in finding new combinations from pre-existing elements', but in a much wider and more profound sense than had been proposed by Durand and steering clear of submission to a single model.

A few years later, with similar theoretical presupposition, Henri Labrouste would renovate the architecture of the day by resolutely introducing the new iron technology, adapting it however to traditional historic models.[10] The supposed opposition between Classical and medieval models seems to resolve itself in Labrouste's buildings by means of the introduction of exposed cast-iron structures. In their slenderness in contrast to

K F SCHINKEL, GARDENER'S HOUSE, CHARLOTTENHOF, POTSDAM

doubt Karl Friedrich Schinkel, whose version of eclecticism was based on suitability or adaptation.[9] His great Ionic colonnade in the Altes Museum where he sought to evoke the eminently cultured 'character' of a museum with its Hellenistic origin, is indisputably one of the most beautiful buildings of the 19th century and one of the closest approximations to the Greek model in the history of architecture. Likewise the Neo-Gothic Church on the Werdersche Markt evokes the Hanseatic tradition of the Middle Ages to which Berlin belonged. In his proximity to rural vernacular models evoked in his picturesque constructions at Gleinicke and the Gardener's House at Charlottenhof, Schinkel developed a more flexible composite system whilst at the same time establishing some permanent bases for the discipline (the 'primitive hut'). In this 'rustic' context, architectonic patterns are simplified and essentialised but, at the same time, Classical fragments reappear in the form of 'genealogical references', taken literally from ancient models and freely superimposed on new buildings. It is a matter of 'decanting' what is essential from what is accessory or ornamentation, although it seems somewhat like a forced meeting between the two.

Later, in his final constructions, Schinkel made an attempt at that achievable in stone, the cast-iron gave a new dimension and ratio to pillars and vaults, closer to medieval 'lightness' than the massiveness of Classicism, but in his Bibliothèque Ste Geneviève and in the Bibliothèque Nationale, these architectural elements are contained within a planimetric and walled arrangement typical of Classicism. However, the models for the Bibliotheque Nationale were not precisely orthodox, as they were with the Bibliothèque of Ste Geneviève. The floor was inspired by the Basilica at Paestum and has a dual scheme with a central row of pillars. It also resembles some medieval floors, such as those in the *domus conversorum* in Cistercian monasteries or the Gothic church of the Toulouse Jacobines. Labrouste's choice in this case was related to his intention of both rationalising the construction of a basilican enclosure and adapting it to a distributive programme. But, whatever the reason, his is an authentic invention resulting from a 'combination of models'.

In the Bibliotheque Nationale the introduction of cast-iron pillars supporting vaults falling on to arches, produces a startling effect reminiscent of the diffuse light inside mosques. The large thermal windows and the iconography however (and this is also true for the Bauakademie) enable us to establish references to a non-conventional Classical world, to, for example, pictorial representations of Pompeii.

In short, the 'Romantic Classicism' of Schinkel and Labrouste represents an attempt to adapt the heritage of historical tradition to a new reality, bringing the two models, the Classical and the medieval, together in honour of a synthesis which transcends both. Imitation was not in this case substituted by the new stylistic 'copy', as occurred in much of the more conventional eclectic architecture of the 19th century, subject as it was to successive revivals. Instead, it continued to be a process of exploring architectonic reality by means of historical models understood in their most general profound sense.

Imitation in the early 20th century

The first half of this century saw the final turning-point with regard to the unity of Classical thought in architecture. This came about not only because of the crisis in the system of Classical orders, but also through the appearance of an architectural avant-garde which was to shatter all the artistic and pedagogical foundations of Classicism. From this moment on we cannot rightly speak of any real continuity in the 'Classical

and *essential* elements, stands above stylistic versions. Their imitation of models is therefore based not so much on stylistic aspects as on more basic composite aspects, which have been 'adapted' to modern habitation programmes and whose 'character' is required for public or institutional buildings.

This *stricto sensu* traditionalism appears as a criticism of the more superficial and outdated academicism of the previous century. To a certain extent, in its return to craftsmanship and the vernacular, it is a continuation of the end of century romanticism represented by Muthesius or the Arts and Crafts movement. However, it also recaptures the representational values of architecture, evoked by Schinkel.[13] Hence in all these works references prevail to 'diverse models' picked out in general from the history of the nation. At the same time, a desire for essentialism is present which, in the case of Asplund, would lead him to explore his own routes to modernity, culminating in the stunning Enkede Crematorium.[14]

The principle of imitation in this case enables us to verify the presence throughout history of a combination of possible models essential to the very existence of architecture. At the same time it serves as a guide to and perspective on architecture. But this does

LABROUSTE, *L TO R*: BIBLIOTHEQUE NATIONALE, PARIS; BIBLIOTHEQUE STE GENEVIEVE, PARIS

Project', although we can trace theoretical fragments and, cyclically, a nostalgia for the lost ideal. Classical thought is still evoked whenever there is an attempt to restore a 'disciplinary order', albeit in a restrictive or partial way. In the same way, architects determined to found their ideas on tradition must draw from Classical thought to a greater or lesser degree, whether their 'models' be vaguely Greco-Roman, medieval or even popular.

Classicism can be seen first and foremost as the legitimisation of supra-historical principles, as a pedagogical basis which transcends time and circumstance. It therefore seems natural to seek to 'imitate' former models with a greater or lesser degree of exactitude, through continuity in foundation and paradigm and the attempt to *adapt* 'familiar architecture'[11], as with Tessenow, whose teaching in the Bauakademie during the first half of the century influenced innumerable German architects. His influence can also be seen on architects from other countries, in particular Nordics such as Petersen, Betsen, Thomsen and, to some extent, Asplund and the elder Lewerentz.[12] apart from their stylistic references to Classicism which are always partial they all denote a certain *atavism*, based on a tradition which, through the theme of the home and the constancy of certain characteristic

not mean a threat to the possibilities introduced by new technology, or even to the architectonic 'elements' introduced by the *via figurativa* of the avant-garde. It is more a question of making *suitable* use of them.

In this connection Tessenow's declaration on his use of window or roof types are well-known:

Perhaps Poelzig is right when he asks himself why he continued designing old windows – high and meticulously sub-divided – ratherthan windows which were low and long.

The question is, deep down, why is the one bad and the other good? Seriously, I have to ask myself why ... We possess an ancient and tested tradition in roof building (I am referring in particular to our different experiments with domes and towers). This not only enables us to recognise the value of tradition, but also leads us to measure ourselves up against the roof as an architectural element, to such an extent that it would seem absolutely unjustifiable if we were to completely renounce either the flat roof or the sloping roof ...The act of defending the flat roof, of trying to improve it or, in certain instances, of choosing it so to speak for its negative character, ought to seem normal to any architect. To think however that the flat roof will, in short, win on all fronts is to undervalue the sloping roof . . . [15]

Tessenow like Schinkel and Labrouste before him was both 'eclectic' and 'critical'. Although a defender of tradition, he was open to innovations when they proved useful.

On the subject of this return to principles to the imitation of models consecrated by tradition mention must also be made of some of the buildings constructed by Behrens in the early decades of the century, especially his work for AEG. Behrens sought to lay the foundations of a typologically new architecture, in terms of tradition, imitating the great monumental architecture of the past but cleverly adapting it to new programmes and technologies. To recapture a monumental likeness in an industrial pavilion was not an easy task if at the same time it meant resisting all temptation to be formalist or picturesque. Behrens was most successful in his AEG manufacturing complex in Berlin, where his architecture displays a new convergence between the Hanseatic Gothic tradition and Classical references, represented respectively in its brickwork and in its immense urban colonnades. However, in contrast with Schinkel or with the more recent work of Tessenow and the Nordics, the ornamentation here is based on the construction, rather than being an after-thought.

It is through works like these that architectural language is revitalised and, at the same time, how a reference to the past is established which does not conflict with innovations in technology. This is even more evident in the Turbinen Fabrik, where the imitation of Classical proportions and composition is at the same time identifiable with an innovative technology, apparent in the details of its structure.

These processes, which consist in translating traditional, Classical models into a technological likeness, also relate to some of Mies Van der Rohe's ideas, such as the Museum of Berlin. His 'virtual canopy' which encloses the Schinkel Museum – defined by four great angular pilasters and an imposing architrave round the four facades of the building – once converted into a tectonic element is conjured up on an enormous stone platform. Mies' complete intuition in this case can only be taken as imitation *in extremis*, completely radical and partial but also conclusive evidence of a constant presence: it is, once again, architraved architecture culturally linked to Classicism and, in this case, to the Romantic Classicism of Schinkel.

JEFFERSON, UNIVERSITY OF VIRGINIA, CHARLOTTESVILLE

Notes

1 Quatremère de Quincy, *De l'imitation*, 1823, facsimile edition, Brussels, 1980.

2 Quatremère de Quincy, *Dictionnaire de l'Architecture*, Paris, 1832.

3 *ibid*.

4 J Rykwert, *On Adam's House in Paradise*.

5 Quatremère de Quincy, *Dictionnaire, op cit*.

6 R Fréart de Chambray, *Parallèle de l'architecture antique et de la moderne*, Paris, 1650.

7 J N L Durand, *Précis des leçons d'Architecture*, Paris, 1819.

8 N Le Camus de Mezières, *Le génie de l'architecture ou l'analogie de cet art avec nos sensations*, Paris, 1780. See also the definition 'Caractère' in Quatremère de Quincy's *Dictionnaire, op cit*.

9 J I Linazasoro, 'Vitrubio en la Modernidad o la reconstrucción del órden perdido' in *Fragmentos* 8 and 9, Madrid, 1986.

10 *ibid*.

11 J I Linazasoro, *El Proyecto Clásico en Arquitectura*, Barcelona, 1981.

12 AAVV, *Clasicismo Nórdico*.

13 See also D Porphyrios, 'Reversible faces: Danish and Swedish architecture 1905-1930', *Lotus* 16, Milan, 1977.

14 H Ahlberg, *Gunnar Asplund architect*, Stockholm, 1950.

15 Quoted by G Grassi in his prologue to *Osservazioni elementari sul costruire*, Milan, 1974.

16 A Windsor, *Peter Behrens: Architect and Designer*, London, 1981.

Translated by Valerie Gardiner

———— * ————

JEAN-PHILIPPE GARRIC
The Imitative Being

PERCIER & FONTAINE, VILLAS D'ESTE AND BORGHESE

The conversation was flowing during dinner until talk turned to the fine arts and someone, in a flush of enthusiasm, brought up the idea of imitation, so causing the abrupt departure from the table of the (otherwise) most courteous architect imaginable ... Each of us has experienced a similar misadventure at some time or another, either as its involuntary instigator or an embarrassed onlooker. And surprising though it may seem, I

believe that the explanation for this kind of behaviour is shame: the conversation had touched upon an act which the fleet-footed individual carried out often, but in secret, in the privacy of their own office.

Imitation is a recourse that architecture has never abandoned. All you need to do to convince yourself of this is take in a little sightseeing in any European city. At Marseilles, for example, a visit to Le Corbusier's *unité d'habitation* followed by a tour of the town's Modern architecture (a dismal day, for sure) confirms the fact that the decades in which the very word 'imitation' was taboo also saw the most mindless plagiarism ever: not even the self-proclaimed and much-copied apostle of invention himself was without guilt in this respect.

While the doctrine of imitation passed down to us from the blessed time of Batteux and Quatremère may have caused some minor squabbles in the past, today it unleashes a storm of passions. Because industrial societies reserve the highest praise and remuneration for the most creative amongst us, there are architects who feel they can glibly dismiss the very idea of imitation but still make themselves masters of the reference, the visual pun, the quotation – indulging in exercises which make a flattering show of their erudition, their sense of irony and *savoir-faire*, while making it quite clear that these are not of paramount importance; rather, the essential thing is their work.

Quatremère understood very early on that architects would soon become preoccupied with showing everyone how clever they were and he used the concept of imitation to counter this vision of a flood of creativity. Yet in spite of all the pages he

devoted to the idea, he never clearly explained what imitation meant in architecture. When he defined it he said that it consisted of 'imitating nature in its methods'. It was a matter, then, of adding to creation using the methods of creation, but he said nothing on this apart from: 'nature does not imitate, but is the object of imitation'.[1]

When he came to illustrate imitation at work he took as his example the ascendance of Greek sculpture, which he described in minute detail in his *Olympian Jupiter* as the emanation, through successive acts of imitation, of God himself – if not in flesh and blood, then at least in ivory and gold – and of Ideal Beauty.

He also defined imitation negatively, saying that it was not copying, that it was to be distinguished from the reproduction found in the practical arts, and that it had nothing to do with the kind of imitative analogies which turned, say, the folds of a robe into fluting, or kiss-curls into Ionic volutes: these were, in his eyes, ridiculous fables.

He constantly made a distinction between true imitation and routine imitation. And in the end he broke with Laugier, upset that an abbot could still, after the passage of so many centuries, prefer a primitive hut to the brilliant works of the masters.

In fact the source of Quatremère's strength and contemporary appeal is this absence of a system. That he lacked one has to be attributed either to his naturally conservative inclinations or to a natural lucidity about theory acquired through reading Condillac.[2] This second possibility would at least have taught him to prefer the diversity and complexity of data resulting from experimentation to the most brilliant of systems. In his *Treatise on Animals*, Condillac wrote: 'Is it therefore so difficult to generalise without the benefit of either accuracy or precision? Is it so difficult to take an idea at random, extend it, and make a system out of it?'[3]

Condillac went further and wrote in defence of the idea that imitation was the special attribute of man: 'Man ended up being so different only by virtue of the fact that he started out as a mimic, and continues to be so; and the reason why animals of a single species don't all act in the same manner is that they don't have the same ability to copy that we do, their society is not capable of those acts of progress which vary both our condition and our conduct.'[4]

This opinion was echoed by Quatremere in the first paragraph of his essay on the nature, aim and means of imitation in the fine arts when he wrote: 'the imitative faculty is truly characteristic of Man: it features in all his acts, it enters into all his works, it is so much a part of him and him alone amongst all creatures, that one could define him through this attribute, naming him: the imitative being.'[5]

While denigrating Kirker, Montfaucon, Gori, Gaylus and others for not sharing his dislike of systems, Quatremere noted that, on the contrary, 'The scholarly Winckelmann [was] the first to bring a true spirit of observation to this study ... the first to discover the principles of criticism and a method which, in putting an end to many errors, opened the way for the discovery of a great number of truths.'[6] And, further, 'I've always observed that in these matters, the negative proof was the easiest to establish: it's easier to say what beauty is not than to say what it is.'[7]

However, we should not be misled by this aversion to systems and insistence on the notions of criticism and negative proof into thinking that Quatremère was a sceptic. He believed in the social necessity and political force of the work of art. He said 'One would therefore term "necessary" those works which have a fixed and determined goal, an application so positive that the maker is obliged to imprint it with a special character. This forces the viewer to find that the work conforms to the reasons behind its production, and gives the public a uniform and precise impression of it.'[8]

Thus, although it was tempting to describe a system of imitation, Quatremère did not do so, but instead applied himself to specifying the best kind of framework for its development. He was convinced that the more necessary elements contributed to the development of the arts of imitation, the better the results, in terms of both their constitution and reproduction.[9]

This writer's confidence in objects was such that he was prepared to say than one could learn more by comparing sublime objects with imperfect ones than one could by visiting galleries containing only prestigious works. 'Even the inferior works of antiquity have a demonstrative property when placed alongside excellent ones, an instructive power which masterpieces in isolation cannot provide us with.'[10]

Contrary to Laugier and Durand, who could come up with no examples of perfect buildings as such, only a handful of guidelines as to how one should go about constructing them, Quatremère believed that perfection had been realised many times in the past; it had only to be imitated in the present.

Imitation was for him (as it was for Marmontel) the most natural thing in the world, requiring only that you confound your memory with your imagination. Marmontel felt, quite aptly, that in the final analysis imitating was like choosing a panel of judges for one's work, saying to oneself: what would Palladio, Wren or Gabriel have to say about my design? What judgement would they make of me?

What the theory of imitation confirms is this: a. a work which can be described in a few words is not necessarily a good one; b. even the best theoretical system cannot provide a guarantee against its adherents producing ugly things; c. no form of rationalism takes account of what is beautiful or good in the arts, and finally, d. the sole gauge of works to come are the masterpieces of the past. The theory of imitation was a means not only of challenging each system with a number of exceptions to the rule but also of denying blanket justification to mediocre works.

To be sure, not everything Quatremère said has relevance outside his own century, for sometimes he played the historian or politician. However he was primarily an exile, nostalgic for a time immemorial when the countryside was prosperous and peaceful, the temples radiant, and the cities free and harmonious. His country was not so much Greece, which he did not know, as Italy, whose land was adorned with ruined temples and villas which had seemingly come straight out of Percier and Fontaine's *Selection of the Most Famous Country Houses in Rome and its Environs*. The inhabitants of this land were his neighbours, and they spent their time imitating nature and beauty on the one hand, and the Divine on the other. While architecture still contains an element of poetry and desire, we cannot help but admire this aesthete who tried to oppose his spirit to the history of art and whose heart broke when he saw that he had failed.

The divide between the kingdom of the fervent and the land of the sceptic is a thin one and Quatremère crossed over often, at least one can imagine he did so: first for several years of disillusion and then for ever in 1831, when he decided to live out his remaining years in quiet obscurity. At what point did he decide to leave an age which bore too close a resemblance to the one he had experienced in a dream – like the saint-to-be experiences hell – at the outset of his career? After 1831, he became like a phantom, with a body that was almost a hundred years old and a spirit that was worn out, but to the end he never sold his soul.

Translated by P Johnston

Notes

1 *Essai sur la nature le but et les moyens de l'imitation dans les Beaux-Arts*, Treuttel et Wurtz, Paris, 1823/AAM, Brussels, 1980, p 4.

2 Etienne Bonnot, Abbé de Condillac, (1714-1780) was the author, amongst other things, of the *Essai sur l'origin des connaissances humaines* (1749) and the *Traité des Sensations* (1754). His work has once again come to the forefront of contemporary debate with the publication by Jacques Derrida of a major essay entitled *l'Archéologie du frivole, Lire Condillac*, Denoel Gonthier, Paris, 1971, and a re-editing, by Michel Serres, of the *Traité des Sensations*, Fayard, Paris, 1984.

3 Condillac, *Traité des Animaux*, Paris, 1755; new edition Fayard, Paris, 1984.

4 *ibid.*

5 Quatremère de Quincy, *op cit*, p 2.

6 Quatremère de Quincy, *Lettres sur le préjudice*, etc, Paris, 1795, p 29.

7 *ibid*, pp 43-4.

8 *Considérations morales sur la destination des ouvrages de l'Art*, Crapelet, Paris, 1815, p 2.

9 *ibid*, p 8.

10 *ibid*, p 30.

---*---

ROBERT ADAM
The Paradox of Imitation and Originality

ROBERT ADAM, WEST WALK HOUSE, SALISBURY

Robert Adam here underlines the absurdity of Modernism's eulogising of avant-garde novelty and its rejection of all previous architectural styles that sought to emulate the past and argues that all buildings inevitably express something of the age in which they are built. Defending the principle of historical inspiration, he says that, paradoxically, it is looking at the past, drawing on earlier models, that can be the source of true originality.

Architectural criticism is cluttered with undefined assumptions and illogical suppositions. In an atmosphere of rational debate these might be harmless enough but in the emotional atmosphere of current architectural sectarianism this lack of clear thinking can close the minds of credulous students and practitioners alike. Chief amongst these ill-considered concepts is the pejorative meaning of the word 'pastiche', which is used to summarise all that species of architecture and design that does not appear to strive to be obviously contemporary, which owes its inspiration and formal expression to a past style, and which lacks that particular quest for originality and overt modernity that – so the story goes – makes a building 'of its time'.

These words 'pastiche' and 'not of its time' are the linchpins of much critical opposition to the well-established and increasing development of direct historical, and generally Classical, inspiration in new architecture. Like all ideas in common currency, the concept of new buildings that are of our time, as contrary to new buildings that are not of our time, carries with it certain conclusions that are not often fully appreciated by exponents of the idea.

In general terms, it is the historical origin of certain building forms which is said to exclude them from that form of contemporary architecture dubbed 'of our time'. The argument goes something like this: certain building forms evolve around a set of historical circumstances and functions specific to their period. They also derive from a response to the current level of building technology and the availability of materials. If these factors change then their formal architectural representation ceases to

have any validity. This seductively simple view has the unfortunate consequence of forcing its exponents to reject much of the architecture of the past.

Architectural history is dominated by, some would say created by, a persistent desire to recreate some period of the past. To say that direct borrowing from and a desire to formally emulate the past is in principle artistically invalid would remove Roman, Romanesque, Renaissance, Baroque, Palladian, Neo-Classical, Gothic Revival, Arts and Crafts, and debatably many more architectural epochs from serious artistic consideration.

Once this point is fully comprehended it is bound to create a considerable dilemma for all but the most extreme opponents of the use of historical inspiration and form in contemporary architecture. A rejection of most, if not all, of the architecture of the past as artistically invalid even at the time it was built is a very difficult attitude to sustain. The origin of this dilemma lies to a significant extent in the 20th-century projection of the 19th-century idea of the avant-garde artist. The fact that much art, later commonly regarded as great, had not found immediate appreciation with the general public (the general public becoming significant only in the 19th century) led by an illogical extension to the view that in order to be *great* art had to be unacceptable to the general public. This enabled and still enables artists (and architects) to feel safe in ignoring public opinion and has brought about the view that the key to being 'of our time' (or slightly ahead of it) lies in the continuous search for a novelty that will surprise and astonish the common man by overturning all those things to which he had become accustomed.

When combined with theories of revolution and a new mythology of technology this view became an essential part of Modernism. So the idea that two species of new art could exist became firmly established: one described as 'of our time' – apparently an accurate reflection of the spirit of its age as perceived and justified only by the avant-garde artist – and the other described as 'not of our time' – taking its inspiration and means of expression from the past and betraying the supposed duty of the artist to forge new artistic frontiers.

The art-historical dilemma created by this idea, which we have already identified, reveals other problems. Even if we do accept the extreme and revolutionary view that Renaissance art and architecture, for example, was a betrayal of a true and presumably Gothic spirit of the 15th century, we are faced with the fact that not only was it actually created but that it did, in fact, very accurately reflect the prevailing climate of humanistic revival of interest in antiquity. Renaissance art did, therefore, express something of the spirit of its particular historical period.

The same fact can be applied to modern buildings. Any building erected today, regardless of what it looks like, expresses some aspect of modern society and is, in this sense at least, a building 'of our time'. A distinctive class of buildings 'of our time' cannot, therefore, be a reference to their *capacity* for expressing something of contemporary culture. The definition must then apply to some underlying idea in the mind of the designer which is expressed through the appearance of the building – in other words, its style.

A lot of claptrap is talked about the idea of style. It is said in some quarters to be a suspect concept in itself, but the simple truth is that once we have established that a collection of buildings possesses recognisable features that relate the members of the collection more to one another than to any other group of buildings we have identified a style. This applies to Baroque and Rococo as much as to Brutalism and High-Tech. Style, quite simply, may be defined as a consistency of combination of those elements which the architect is free to manipulate in the design of a building.

We all know that architectural elements can be combined in various ways which will give certain specific impressions to certain specific types of people. It is possible, by a combination of these elements, to make a new building remind certain people of a type of existing building or even of one specific existing building. Indeed, this is the means by which almost all modern architects, in common with architects of all periods, associate themselves with particular contemporary architectural movements – often consciously, through the influence of publications and buildings, and just as often unconsciously.

We can go further and say that very few, if any, buildings are wholly original or novel in conception or appearance. Con-structional necessity, function and the perceptual process guarantee that this will always be the case. Some buildings are, without doubt, relatively more unusual or more influential than others, but all architects are influenced by other architects, artists or designers. Distinct architectural movements tend to have their roots in other architectural, artistic or cultural movements.

While the principle of progressive stylistic development may hold, it is also clear that all buildings are original and individual regardless of their debt to other buildings. Not only are highly imitative buildings (such as the many derivations of the Farnsworth House) quite different in their setting and in aspects of their planning, but the fact that their style is distinctly dependent on an original makes them conceptually different from that original building – which could not be stylistically dependent on itself.

Although apparently a rather delicate point, this relationship between originals and derivations has some significance in understanding the creative position of historically inspired design. If we apply it to the Gothic Revival or to Neo-Classicism, for example, we can see quite clearly that, in spite of (and really because of) a designer's desire to recreate, Gothic Revival and Neo-Classical buildings are characteristic of their own era and, as such, are quite different from the buildings and styles they sought to emulate.

This now puts us in a position to combine two of our conclusions: first that *originality and individuality are to a significant degree inevitable*, and second that *complete stylistic or visual novelty are in practice unachievable*. It will follow that originality is not dependent on novelty. Or, put another way, as almost all buildings are to a degree stylistically dependent on other buildings, the fact that an architect chooses to associate himself with a particular style does not mean that he is abandoning his capacity for originality. To this we can add our earlier conclusion that *any building erected in a particular period must express something relevant to that period.* (Indeed, the greater the number the greater the relevance). Thus we can conclude finally that drawing inspiration and formal expression directly from historic architecture does not of necessity lessen the possibilities for achieving originality and modernity.

Anyone seriously engaged in designing historically derived buildings will know this from everyday practice, and yet it is consistently denied by critics on the basis of the logically flawed idea that there is a class of buildings not 'of their time' which are thereby automatically open to the charge of pedantry and plagiarism. It is hoped that the conclusions drawn here will not only help to demonstrate the redundancy of that concept but will help us to understand the relationship between historic style and historically derived style and thereby contribute to constructive debate on the use of history in contemporary architecture.

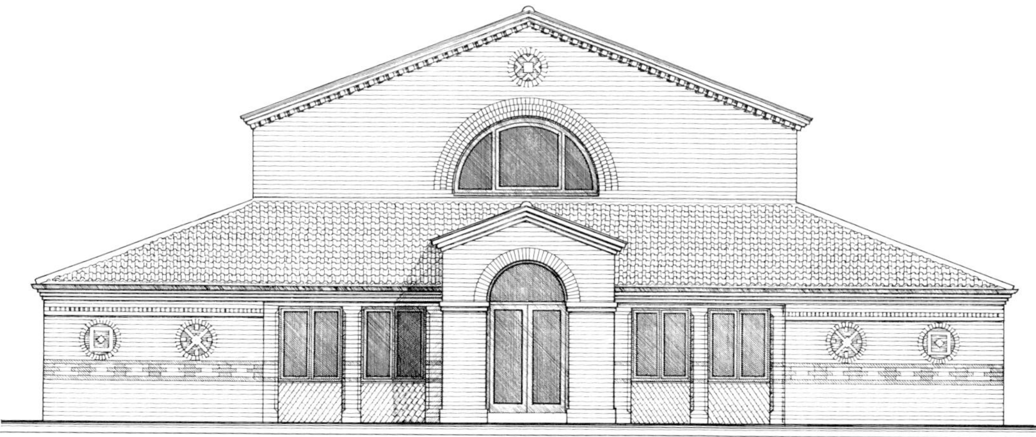

ROBERT ADAM WITH EVANS, ROBERTS & PARTNERS, BORDON LIBRARY, HAMPSHIRE

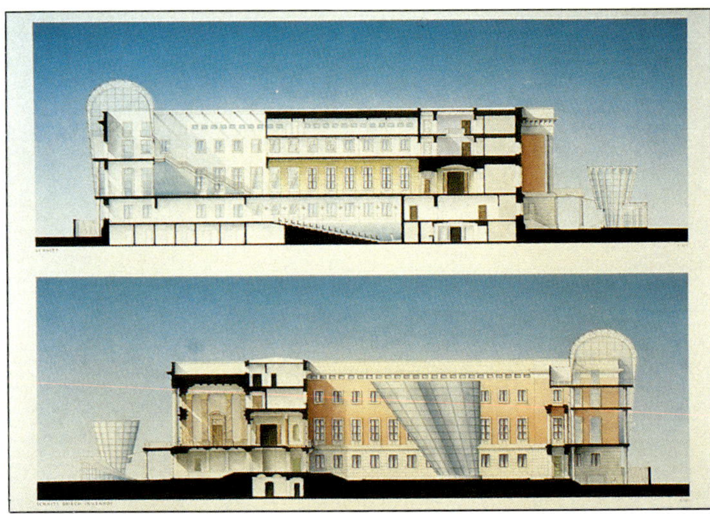

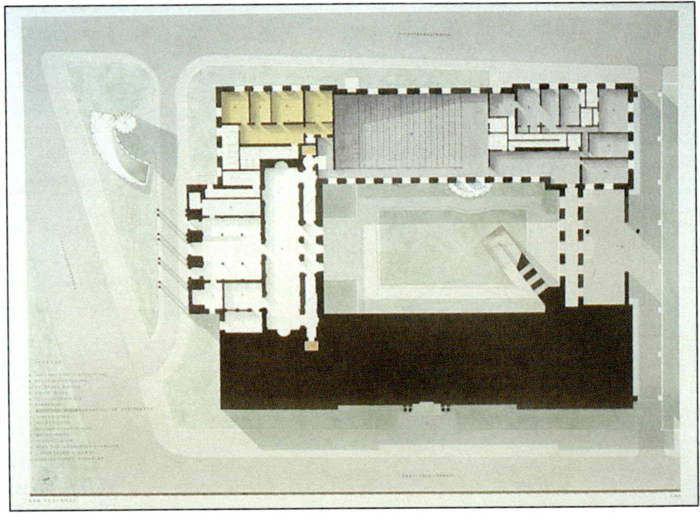
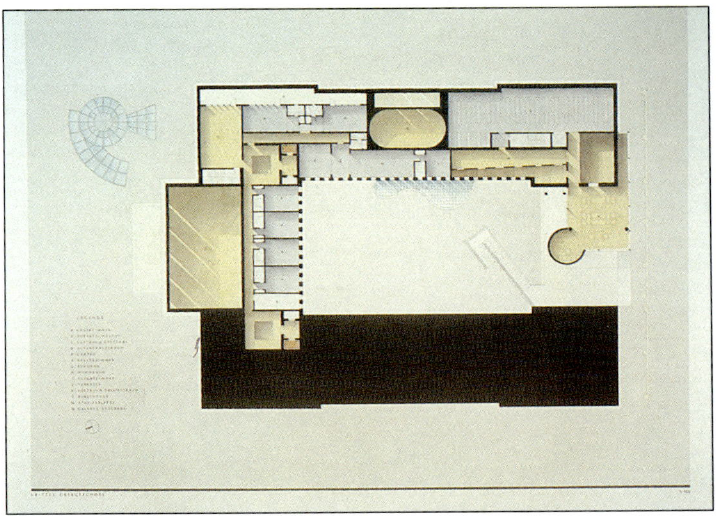

ACADEMY OF SCIENCE, BERLIN: ELEVATIONS, SECTIONS, PLANS AND PERSPECTIVE

ROBERT STERN
Design as Emulation

OBSERVATORY HILL DINING HALL, UNIVERSITY OF VIRGINIA

As an architect, it has been my privilege to build in places where inherited and borrowed forms have been successfully cross-pollinated with deep-rooted local traditions, places that are, as a result, intimately related to the shared values which form the essence of a common culture. For the most part, in an effort to sustain and even enlarge upon a sense of place, I have tried to build up the fabric of prevailing local, fundamentally traditional

architectural culture, whether in the city or the country. Beyond issues of function and tectonics, architecture is an act of representation and, whilst there are a number of things that building can appropriately represent, for me the fundamental subject is 'place', which I define as the physical continuum that the new building is to be part of and is, as such, obliged to enhance. But to imitate a particular site's context does not mean succumbing to a simple notion of stylistic replication or that past modes of expression can be pursued in a 'natural' way, as though the machine and a hundred other circumstances of contemporary culture and architectural production had not made them alien from typical, everyday building. For me, the design process is one of emulation; combining imitation and invention. I work with a knowledge of and a sympathy for the past, but I endeavour not to confuse the circumstances of our era with that of another. I begin with what is already there, but I try not to let myself be found by it. In this respect I am a Modern architect, if not necessarily a Modernist.

In many of my designs, I have drawn upon the building tradition of Boston's shore towns, which lead from the 17th-century salt-box to the late 19th-century houses that constitute what Vincent Scully has labelled 'the Shingle Style'. The supple variety possible within this hybrid mode, and its extraordinary capacity to respond to the particular sites and social mores of the northeast coastal areas, continues to fascinate me and refresh my work. So it is that in recent houses similar circumstances of site could lead to related but sharply divergent designs. The Hardscrabble House and the Marblehead House both combine a

rough, stone base and a shingled superstructure, rendering them complementary to their natural settings. Their plans and volumetric expressions grew out of considerations of sloping sites leading to spectacular views. But whereas the property was regular and the view faced south and west at the Hardscrabble House, at Marblehead the lot was irregular, the neighbours' sight lines needed to be guaranteed and the northerly view made us want to backlight important rooms. The result was far more picturesque than at Hardscrabble as we struggled to literally grab for the sun.

The Shingle Style, while not exactly a vernacular, has enough of the purely local about it to make the process of emulation relatively easy to justify for an architect still wrestling in his inner soul with the near-ineradicable values of a Modernist education and an 'art-culture' that still seems to hold innovation in higher esteem than invention, and boldness over refinement. Thus, it has been a slow, ongoing process for me to come to terms with Classicism, that is until I was asked to build at the University of Virginia. To work in the Classical tradition in America requires a recognition of Jefferson's achievement, because he was the first to articulate tradition's place in a culture that, at some levels at least, considers itself distinct from the past. Through Classical architecture, Jefferson hoped to liberate American architecture from the immediate English and European past, yet bind it to the traditions of ancient Greece and Rome, to the continuum of Western civilisation as a whole. His University of Virginia campus is a paradigm for American architecture: its genius is not in the specific elements taken from the Classical tradition, but in the way the elements are put together. For Jefferson, American architecture did not consist of a new language, but it did engage a struggle to say new things.

The Observatory Hill Dining Hall at the University of Virginia in Charlottesville (1982-4) was my first significant building that was not a house. Its setting and the specific requirements of the programme combined to be an extraordinary challenge. On the surface, the mandate was to add 200 seats to a 10-year-old dining hall and to renovate the interior; behind that was a challenge to help reaffirm a neglected past. In the 1950s to 1970s, the University's building programme was immersed in the anti-situational enterprise of non-representational, a-contextual Modernism. I was invited to build at Charlottesville as part of Dean Jaquelin Robertson's programme to effect a rapprochement between the university's building policies and its Jeffersonian traditions. My decision to 'wrap' the existing dining hall in Classical architecture was influenced in part by Louis Kahn's ideas about wrapping buildings in ruins to elevate the ordinary to the heights of architecture. At Observatory Hill, I tried to wrap what I saw as a ruin of architecture in an exaltation of Classical order and light, to put back what the previous architect had

to a commanding view across a long sloping meadow. On the cross-axis of the house a second stair descends to a grass terrace that widens as it leads west to rolling lawns beyond, an idea adapted from George Howe's High Hollow (1941).

Each of the projects so far presented in this discussion have had a domestic character and domestic scale. In these, traditional language could be spoken with a degree of authenticity; the buildings could be built pretty much as they had been in the past, and the scale and purposes of the rooms differ only in degree.

But what of buildings of vastly larger scale, and more importantly, conceived for purposes and realised in materials wholly distinct from the past? What of loft-like office buildings, for example, perhaps the foremost architectural problem of the post-industrial age? Issues of tradition and modernity have thus far nowhere come to greater focus for me than on the office building now being designed for Boston. 222 Berkeley Street is my first urban office tower – not only the characteristic 20th-century American building type, but to be realised on an extensively debated and widely contested site. The challenge posed by 222 Berkeley Street, a mixed-use building in Boston's Back Bay combining offices, shops, a winter garden and underground car

L TO R : HARDSCRABBLE HOUSE, MARBLEHEAD HOUSE

apparently chosen to leave out. The new additions ally the facility to the Jeffersonian tradition by the intimate scale of the four metaphoric 'porches', and their clearly defined base, middle and top. The steel and glass screen wall and glazed lanterns flood the porches with light, while French windows can open to the fresh air in good weather. Elements such as hipped roofs, arches, moulded brick, white-painted wood columns and trim reinforce the scale and character.

The house in Chestnut Hill, Massachusetts, now under construction, draws on the different New England tradition of late-Georgian Classicism as interpreted by American Federal-era architects, such as Charles Bulfinch, and successfully reinterpreted from the 1890s until the Second World War by innumerable architects. On my mind was nearby Gore Place. Built in 1806 to the design of the French architect Jacques-Guillaume Legrand and the owner, John Gore, it sits on the crest of a hill, resulting in a distinct sense of front and back. So, too, the Chestnut Hill house, set at the end of a cul-de-sac which it embraces with wings and flanking pavilions to form a motor court. An axial sequence leads past an open stair-hall and dining room to the vaulted living room that opens through a glass wall

parking, was to produce a building that could successfully operate in the marketplace, yet fit in with one of the most elaborate yet fragile urban contexts in America, which with the construction of large office buildings along Boylston Street and facing Copley Square has been dramatically altered in a way that seems to many observers to be destructive.

In response to strong community concerns for a design with a distinctly Bostonian and Back Bay character, 222 Berkeley is clad in red brick and trimmed in granite. In order to make its contextual intentions more explicit, the Georgian vocabulary of 18th- and early 19th-century Boston architecture becomes the basis for the exterior expression; a vocabulary that was highly regarded in the late 19th and early 20th century as well, when buildings such as McKim Mead & White's Browne and Meredith Apartment Building (1890-91) facing the Common and the large, locally admired Ritz-Carlton Hotel (Strickland, Blodget and Law, 1927) were undertaken. Bay windows at street level and the floors above refer to the typical late 19th-century townhouses of the Back Bay and the small-scale retailers nearby, as well as the Coulton Building (1905), which formerly stood on the site. The elaborate Classical details for the Boylston Street entrance,

22

which is flanked by paired columns carrying urns and entered through a revolving door housed in a tempietto, emphasise the public importance of this entrance. A variation on 18th-century orangeries, and on Boston's widely admired Horticultural Hall (Wheelwright and Haven, 1901), crowns the office tower, offering a distinct skyline silhouette that places it firmly within the American tradition of Classical skyscrapers.

Given my concern for the American context, and the need to see architecture in broader cultural and stylistic terms than was typical a generation ago, observers abroad may quite rightly ask whether such an approach could be translated to a non-American context. It cannot be denied that while Americans are obsessed with the past precisely because they have so very little of it to call their own, Europeans quite oppositely and understandably to an extent feel smothered by it. So what would be an appropriate response to a European context for an American architect interested in culturally contextual design?

The Mexx Headquarters in Holland, my first building abroad, offers some answers. It consists of a completely reconstructed 125-year-old landmark building that once belonged to a company of silversmiths, and a new building that virtually doubles

ten (Academy of Science) in Berlin, the differences between American and European attitudes towards the past became critical. To begin with there was the disturbing context of a Classical building designed in the late 1930s for an unpalatable political purpose. As I saw it, our task was not to restore the former Italian embassy to its previous physical and conceptual integrity, but to challenge that integrity. To do this, the proposal turns to the materials (glass and metal) and the forms (dynamic abstract shapes) which most closely represent the ideal of science as a process of renewal, and whose symbolism challenged the static monumentality of Friedrich Hetzelt's design.

I based our design on a belief that our future in large part depends on the ability of the science community to work within the public realm, a belief to which architecture is powerfully able to give expression. Therefore I felt it essential to infuse the programme with symbols that, given the repressive history of the host building, would convey a new sense of it as home to an open institution in a democratic society; to make bold new shapes function as instrumentalities of the democratic order, while leaving to the existing, traditional elements their function as containers of ceremony; to acknowledge a particular past and a tradition

L TO R : CHESTNUT HILL HOUSE, 222 BERKELEY STREET, BOSTON

the facilities. It struck me that only a Modernist response was appropriate. Not an ahistorical, putatively astylar design, but one which recognised that Modernism, in all its variety, can be seen as a tradition within the larger Modern tradition of architecture that began with the Renaissance. Thus, while I didn't imitate the immediate context, I did respond to it in a specifically Dutch Modernist tradition. The design is a homage to that aspect of Dutch Modernism imbued with a slightly mad, almost surreal quality. There was a moment in the 1930s when this sensibility was synthesised with that of Classicism, as in the work of S van Ravestyn, designer of Rotterdam Zoo (1937-41) among many fascinating works. I tried to capture the spirit of this moment, to give the new Mexx a sense of grandeur and dignity played against an inspiringly mad Modern Classicism.

Our client wanted a large room for parties, fashion shows and as a day-to-day meeting place. The main room created to meet this request is treated as an enclosed courtyard, bound on three sides by self-contained offices and protected from the weather on the fourth by a great, curved, glass wall. The wall is free of the columns and also leans – a literal curtain drawn across the space.

In undertaking a proposal for the Akademie der Wissenschaf-

as well a troubling present and an optimistic ideal for the future. The former embassy rests squarely in the Classical tradition of the Modern era, and despite the political circumstances associated with its construction, the architectural validity of that tradition remains. Yet while I have given scrupulous attention to preservation, it would be irresponsible to simply reconstruct the original building, given its past and its present.

Working in a tradition is, I believe, essential to the making of places, but it has its dangers as well; one can easily be seduced into believing that because traditional architectural languages continue to have meaning, the traditional cultures in which they began also continue to exist, or more naively, can possibly be revived.

The point it seems to me is quite the opposite: the tension between the timeless way of building and the all too-timely circumstances that call a building into being guarantees that a vital architecture will continue, that the tension between the pastness and the presence of the past will foster a new-old architecture more culturally resonant than one that is either all about the past or all about the present. As we meet the obligations of the present, we had better keep faith with the past.

SOUTH ADDITION, END VIEW

ROBERT STERN
Two Recent Projects

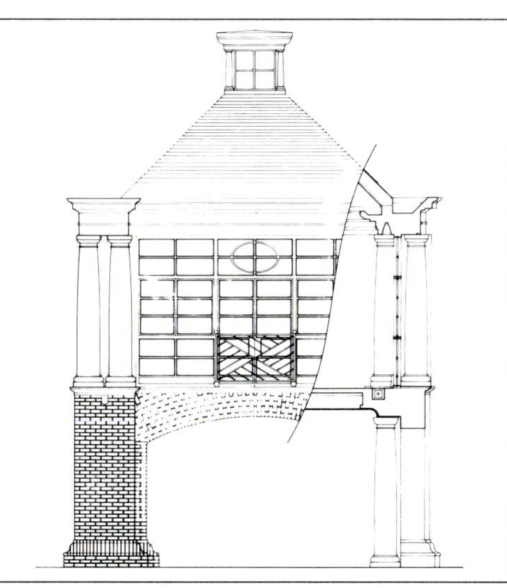

NORTH ADDITION

Observatory Hill Dining Hall

At the University of Virginia campus the plan and architecture render visible the balance between the universal ideal of Classicism and the particular provincial circumstances that are the essential 'regional' realities of American architecture. Jefferson's achievement exemplifies the value of an architecture that begins with imitation and finds its own voice.

The additions to the Observatory Hill Dining Hall are metaphoric porches intended to camouflage the existing facility and ameliorate the disjunction between that building and the university's Jeffersonian architectural tradition. In the most basic terms, the additions give the building a clearly defined base, middle and top, which it has lacked until now and without which it bears no real relation to the traditional architecture of the campus.

The four-bay massing of each porch

ELEVATION AND SECTION DETAIL

addition consciously departs from the dining hall's monolithic character and imparts to it the more intimate scale of Jefferson's Lawn. Inside and out, specific elements, such as hipped roofs, arches, moulded brick, Classical columns and wood trim, have been used to reinforce the scale and character suggested by the overall massing.

The two new wings provide extra seating and a Classical face more appropriate to the setting than the bland 70s block they surround. On the south side, the new wing is raised on a simple brick arcade with paired Tuscan columns. White glazing bars to floor level make the windows a decorative feature, unlike the previous utilitarian plate glass. Internally the dining hall has been refurbished with new furniture, lighting, wooden ceilings and colonnades around the structural columns.

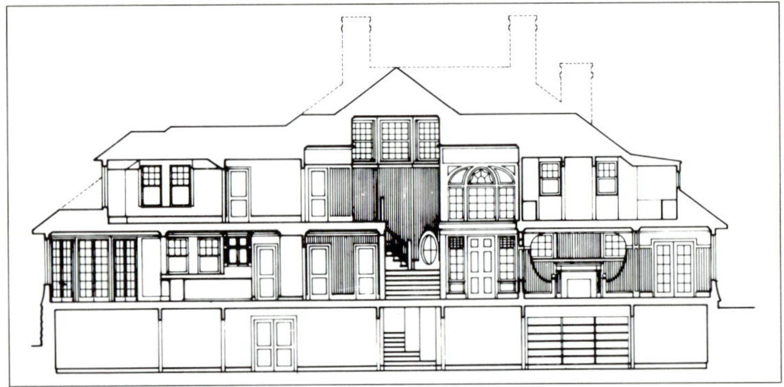 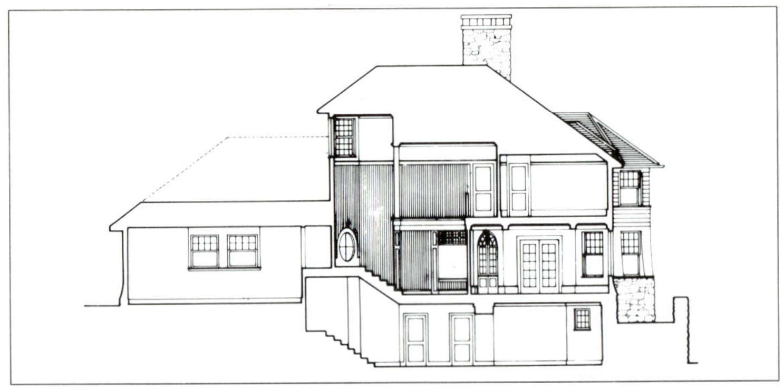

ABOVE L TO R: SECTIONS FACING SOUTHWEST AND SOUTHEAST; *BELOW:* DETAILS

House at Marblehead

Set on a steeply pitched site with northerly views towards the water, this house continues the architectural traditions refined in the stone and timber cottages that dotted Boston's North Shore as well as the rest of coastal New England at the turn of the century. As the land falls away, the house's rubble-stone foundation emerges, a high base anchoring the more finely detailed and picturesquely massed shingled superstructure.

Responsive as it is to the delicate balance required between the requirements for good interior planning, solar orientation and view, the massing of the house – replete with projecting bays and subsumed porches – is rendered formally sensible by a complex network of hipped roofs rising hierarchically to a unifying ridge line, whilst the bays and porches play with effects of light and shade.

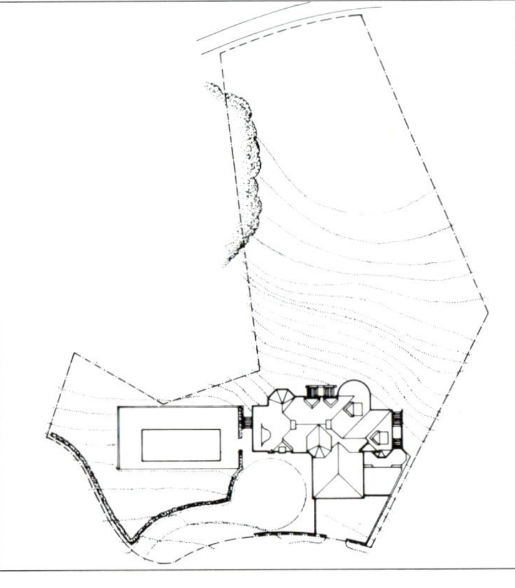

SITE PLAN

An L-shaped plan enhances the house's apparent compactness by lessening its perceived mass at the view side; at the front, this configuration defines an entry precinct separated by high garden walls from a service court. Within, the plan is centred around the interwoven planes and volumes of the cruciform living room, double-height entry hall and turreted stair to foster a relaxed architecture of the interior consonant with the exterior's relative informality.

This example of vernacular architecture shows signs of Arts and Crafts influence in the large, projecting, stone chimney which has become a principle feature of the house, the steeply pitched roofs and the geometric, grid element above the front door. Archways and stone steps create picturesque vistas from the landscaped gardens.

DUANY AND PLATER-ZYBERK
Houses in Texas and Florida

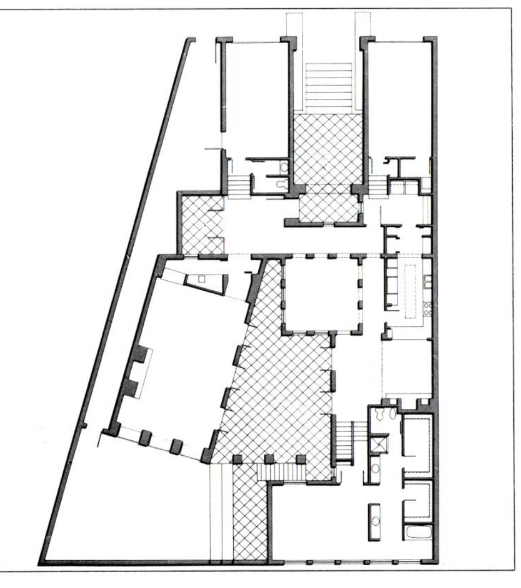

LIVING-ROOM WING AND BEDROOM WING OVERLOOKING GARDEN

Westover House

UPPER-LEVEL PLAN

The programme of the Westover House called for three bedrooms and a two-car garage as well as the usual complement of semi-public rooms. The site was of very narrow frontage, and was further complicated by sloping sharply downhill from the road. The architectural review board of the subdivision in Fort Worth, Texas, prescribed one zero-setback side yard, a constant eaves-line at ten foot above grade, a specific mixed blend of brick and a Classical style.

This design dealt with these requirements in the following manner. The two-car garage, which would have dominated the length of the narrow frontage, was neutralised as a facade element by being split, with a dominant entry court formed in the middle. The slope was absorbed in a series of level exterior spaces, starting with the sunken entry court and followed by two progressively lower podia, each corresponding to a group of interior spaces. The requirement for a constant eaves line, which would have resulted in a roof of little character, was side-stepped by pavilionising the elements, including the entry court where the roof sloped *down* from the required line. The rooms are arranged around the rear courtyard and, as the garages occupy the street frontage, this reversal gives the clients privacy. Simplified, geometric, Classical forms are used in the porticoed, pedimented end facade of the living room.

The specified mixed blend of brick was separated into the component colours, one assigned to the podium elements and the other to the building elements. Construction is within the local vernacular of wood structure with brick cladding and copper roofing.

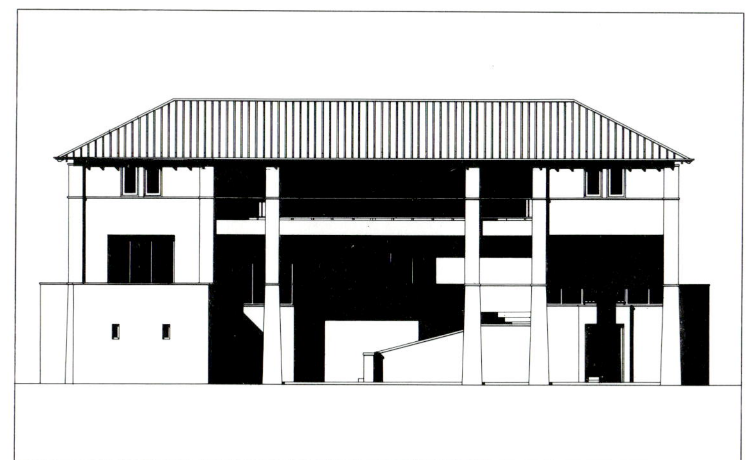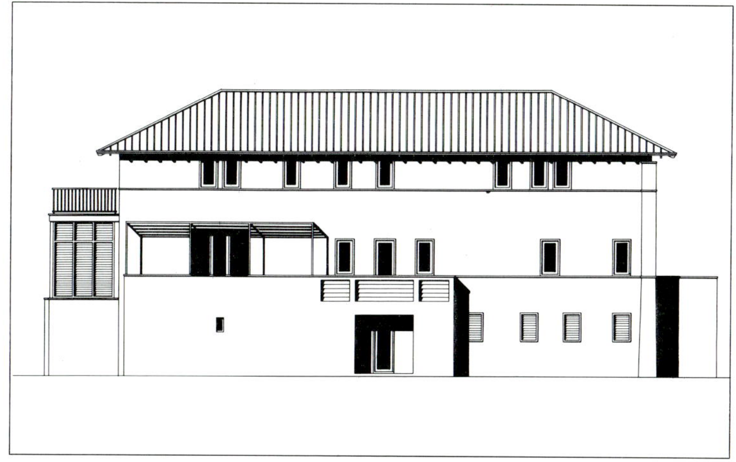

ABOVE L TO R: EAST ELEVATION; SOUTH ELEVATION; *BELOW*: MODEL, WEST ELEVATION

Rosen House

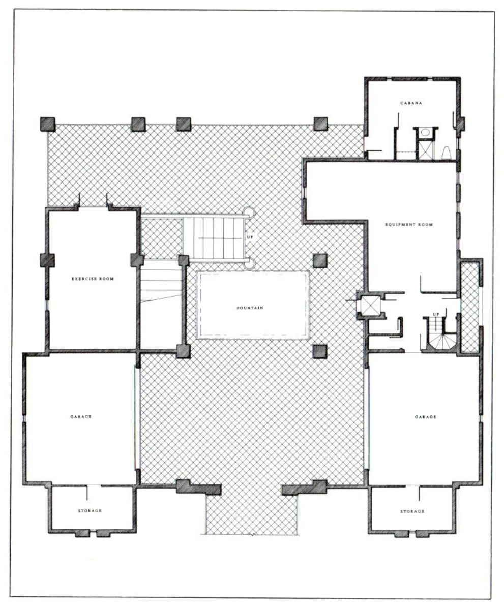

The Rosen House in Miami, Florida, attempts a synthesis of the Classical tradition and Caribbean vernacular architecture. The conditions of the site required that the lowest habitable level be raised a minimum of ten feet above grade. The entrance to the house is shared by both pedestrians and automobiles, leading on to an atrium with garages. The family holds very large social affairs, which will take place at the ground level, in the space of the tropical atrium and in the rear loggia that faces the ocean. Both of these spaces are supported by columns whose proportions are derived from the Royal Palm, which is indigenous to the region and will also be found in the house's gardens.

GROUND-FLOOR PLAN

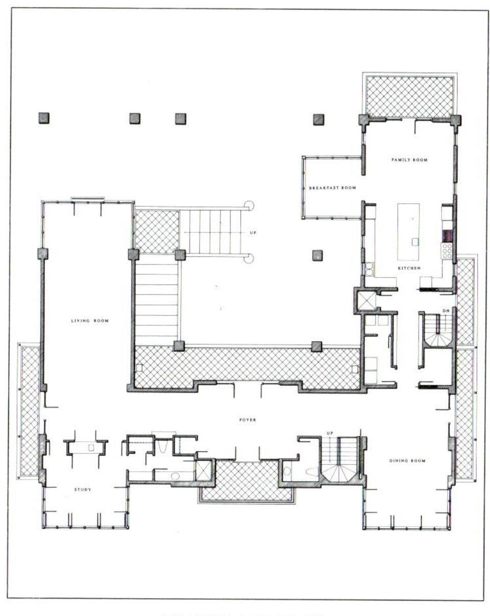

MAIN-FLOOR PLAN

LIAM O'CONNOR
Institute of the Arts Project, Rome

PERSPECTIVE VIEW OF LIBRARY

The project completes an urban block near the Ponte Sisto in Rome. The Institute of the Arts comprises an entry gate into the piazzetta, lecture theatre and octagonal gallery, a large refectory with double-height library above reached by a rotunda, workshops, numerous lecture rooms and a galleried hall for public occasions.

The buildings are organised around a piazzetta and two other courts. The piazzetta gives access to the main functions of the Institute and contains two fountains. One stands on an axis with the entry gate and the library rotunda, the other on an axis with the entrance to the lecture-building court. The two fountains make a symmetrical composition with the monumental Ionic portico. The four piazzetta entrances are closed to the public at night.

The general arrangement of buildings

PERSPECTIVE VIEW OF PORTICO

is the result of using primary room types and by using different architectural treatments to assert their relative functional and symbolic importance within the Institute as well as within the wider context of the city of Rome.

The urban block was not considered as a single building but as a number of simple building typologies which, by their grouping and architecture create a variety of open spaces, rooms, building forms and facades. The hierarchical relationship between the different buildings is thus made legible.

The construction uses traditional materials: columns, entrances, architraves and ground-floor rustication are in the local travertine, while the remaining wall surfaces are in stucco. Roofs are of either copper sheet or terracotta pan- and angle-tiles, window frames are of bronze.

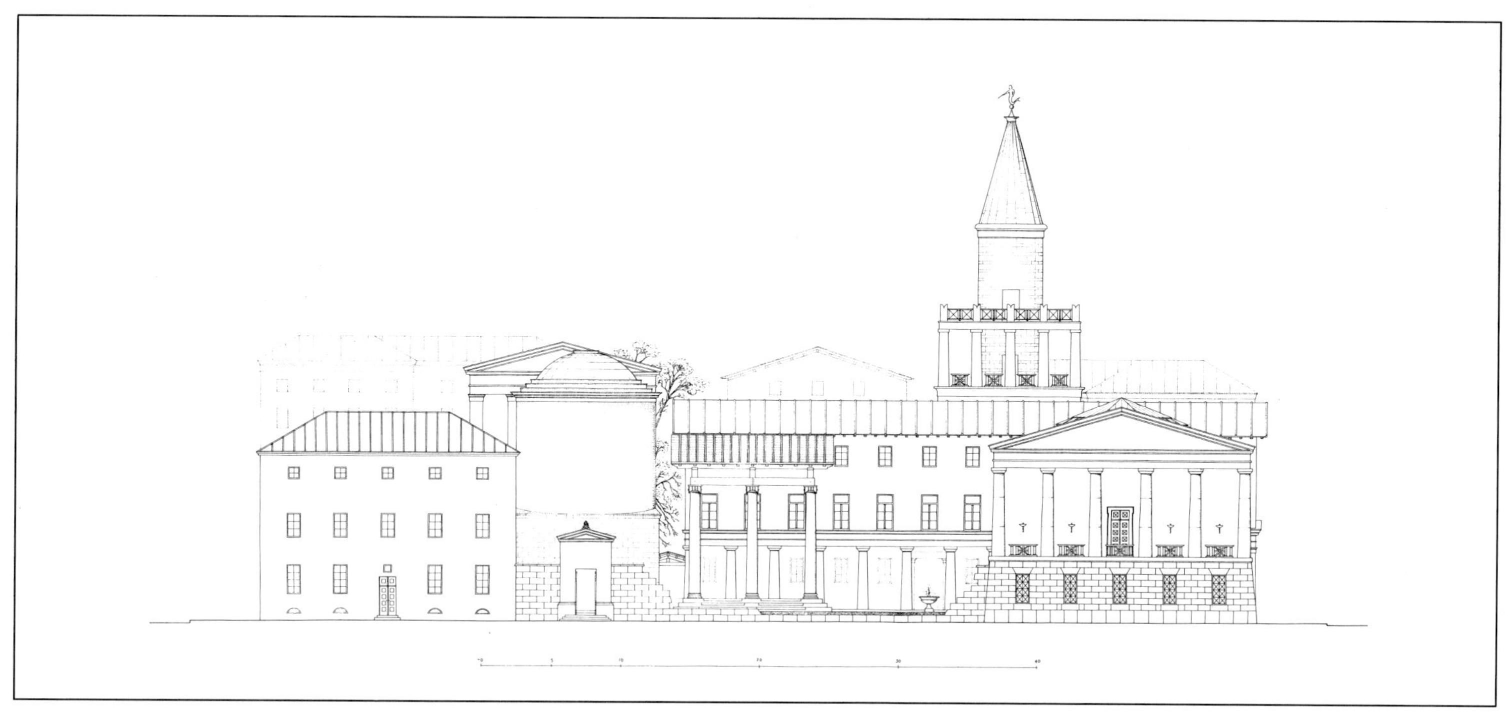

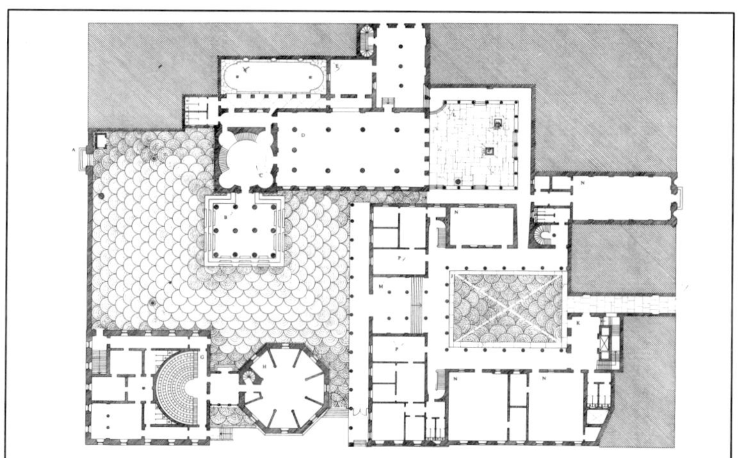

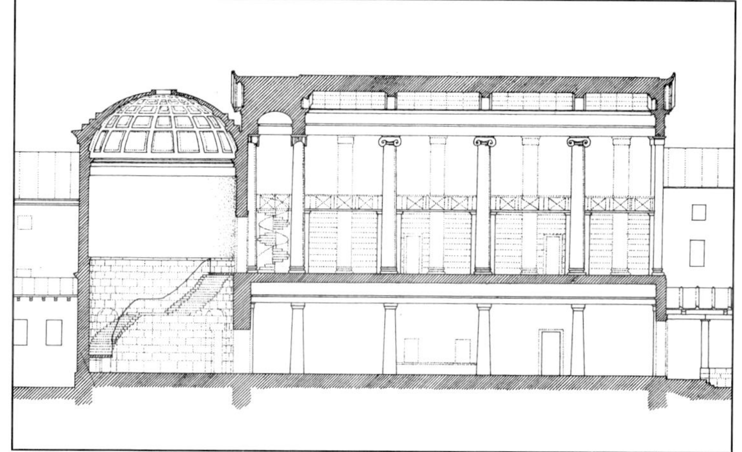

ABOVE: FRONT ELEVATION; *CENTRE L TO R*: GROUND-FLOOR PLAN; LONGITUDINAL SECTION THROUGH LIBRARY; *BELOW*: SIDE ELEVATION

QUINLAN TERRY
Richmond Riverside

RIVERSIDE FRONTAGE

As the last bits of scaffolding wait to be taken down before the royal opening in October, it is now possible to study the overall scheme. At first sight Quinlan Terry's Richmond Riverside is an unusually convincing re-creation of a period piece. This is because rather than choosing to install a single 'Georgian' set-piece, the scheme incorporates a variety of different Classical styles and the use of different Classical orders apertaining to give the impression of different dates and scales – as well as incorporating three existing buildings of architectural merit. On closer inspection keystones and litter bins reveal 1988, behind facades lie office spaces and underground car parking.

A variety of materials have been used to add variety of colour and texture, yellow and red bricks, reconstituted stone, stucco, flint rubble in Water Lane and some fine metal-work detailing in pleasantly simple balconies, railings and gates. Many charges have been levelled against the scheme of pastiche, indeed it does try to give the impression of having always been there or of having evolved, although the 20th-century qualities are apparent. Columns and details are chunky, not just thin detailing as with much Classical revival work. Theories of imitation could seem suspect if, as here, the solution is not one historic style but a mix, but this can also be defended on grounds of giving each building its own character. Terry sees himself as developing an architecture valid for today, 'Classicism . . . is certainly the *natural* way to build'. Local popularity and acceptance in a distinctive part of riverside London have been achieved, and mixed use with flats and shops as well as offices.

RESTAURANT BUILDING, FRONT ELEVATION

ONTAGE; *BELOW*:WHITTAKER SQUARE ELEVATION

ABOVE: VIEW TO RESTAURANT BUILDING AND CASTLE HOUSE; *BELOW*: TOWN SQUARE

ABOVE: HILL STREET ELEVATION; *CENTRE*: RIVERSIDE F

ARCH BETWEEN WHITTAKER SQUARE AND TOWN SQUARE

RIVERSIDE FRONTAGE, THE RESTORED HERON HOUSE AND PALM COURT WITH NEW GATEWAY BUILDING BETWEEN

ALLAN GREENBERG, US DEPARTMENT OF STATE, WASHINGTON

ALLAN GREENBERG
Thoughts on Freedom and Imitation

ALLAN GREENBERG, BLANCH RESIDENCE, FRONT ELEVATION

In the wake of his landmark exhibition of work of students at the French Ecole des Beaux-Arts, organised in 1975 at the Museum of Modern Art in New York, Arthur Drexler described the dilemma of Modernistic architecture: 'Modern architecture ... acknowledges freedom by seeking to embody divergent possibilities, but it has not yet dared to relinquish the reductionist imperatives of the engineering style. Devised to tell the "truth" about

necessity, its form language is now the only language available. And so it happens that the one necessity modern architecture cannot freely confront is the necessity for freedom.'[1] What constitutes the 'freedom' Drexler describes and why is it a 'necessity'? Certainly this freedom could not have meant either the mindless pursuit of architectural novelty for its own sake that preoccupies the avant-garde or the banal buildings so characteristic of much of the construction of the past 50 years.

Drexler's idea of the necessity of freedom grows out of Judeo-Christian usage. Freedom means being released from ties or from bonds of external force(s). It is a state of not being in bondage, of non-slavery, civil liberty, independence or personal liberty. In this sense, it is not a static, easily defined quality but is always measured with reference to some set of bounds or limits. The nature of these bounds is of critical importance for they should create societies that maximise individual freedom. The bounds grow out of moral structures such as mutual non-injury within the group: do not do unto others what you would not have them do to you. Bounds are therefore a precondition for life, liberty and happiness, for creative human enterprise, social intercourse and pursuit of wisdom. Bounds define freedoms and other qualities of life that are valued. They should not place citizens in bondage to individuals, corporations, mobs, interest groups, governments or religions. Therefore, to be free is to voluntarily accept limits on behaviour, or to agree to abide by laws, conventions or sets of moral and ethical standards in the conduct of one's life.

In the United States, the Declaration of Independence, the Constitution and the Bill of Rights provide the framework, accepted by all citizens, with which to establish freedom by limiting the role and responsibilities of government. In the religious sphere, Jews accept the 613 laws, which include the ten commandments, as the moral authority to guide believers to the path of wisdom and to avoid life's shoals. For Christians it is the ten commandments and the New Testament which are the accepted authority. In all these examples acceptance of common bounds or laws and limits on authority (termed a 'yoke' in the Bible) paradoxically liberates both the individual and the group, by defining acceptable behaviour within which social, economic, political and personal goals may be achieved.

A set of such limits commonly held by a group of people creates a common sphere in which language, art, science, politics and urbanism can flourish. Each of these disciplines (the very word connotes limits) has its own set of bounds. Students at university spend most of their time studying the nature of the bounds of the subjects comprising their course of study. These bounds, together with the output of writers, scholars and artists, create our culture. But culture is more than this for it includes not only what we say, or think, but what we do, our deeds. It is a dynamic process in which an idea leads to action, in turn causing reflection and reassessment of the original idea. This sets the process in motion again. In this way, culture is enriched, transformed and modified by incorporating new ideas, ideals and achievements as well as renewing and strengthening older beliefs and ideals. The common bounds or 'yoke' are the essential framework on which this discourse is built.

Tradition is the vehicle by which culture is transmitted from one generation to the next. The very word tradition is defined, in one of its senses, as 'opinion or belief or custom *handed down*'[2] (my italics). Its Latin root *trado* means to *hand on* or deliver, derived from the Hebrew *Masoret*, handing down, the word used to describe the handing down of the laws from God to Moses on Mount Sinai and from Moses to Joshua, to the elders, to the Prophets and on down succeeding generations in an unbroken chain to the present. The process of handing down or handing on specifically avoids any sense of ownership. Tradition is an inheritance which we claim for future generations but do not own.[3] To lose these laws, or any aspect of a tradition, may be a catastrophe for it involves loss of fundamental basics of our common sphere.

The passage, growth and development of tradition over time is best studied by the example of law. Jewish law is the oldest field of law still relevant and in use today. It has two components: written law and oral law. The written law is fundamental and sets forth the basic tenets of the tradition; the oral law explains and interprets the written law in specific circumstances as they arise. American law incorporates a similar two-tier structure founded on the constitution. The body of law related to lower court decisions is less established and incorporates unique aspects of present experience. This is constantly changing and expanding to accommodate new conditions and may, over time, profoundly affect our understanding of the Constitution. American law grows out of Jewish, Roman and English law, all of which are structured on the use of precedent.

This combination of static and dynamic elements is characteristic of a great tradition. Much of what is crucial to a tradition may be written, as in the Magna Carta or the United States' Constitution, but by far the larger and most crucial parts may be embodied in a vast array of unwritten beliefs, assumptions and ideals held in common by a nation or group. There is a continuous interplay between the permanent or more basic portions, and the newer, more dynamic and volatile parts. Changes take place over years, centuries and even millenia. For example, the effort to achieve full democracy and women's rights, on the one hand, has occupied much of documented history. On the other, the establishment of the Marshall Plan and the United Nations took place over a comparatively short period of time. To be traditional, therefore, is by definition to be both alive in the present and connected to the past. Tradition is a living part of our daily existence.

To choose to break with tradition, even in the extreme condition of a revolution, is fraught with danger for it is easy to lose orientation and reference, as occurred in the French and Russian revolutions, and exchange one form of bondage for another. The more conservative English and American revolutions avoided this tragedy. At a personal level, rejection of tradition has similar pitfalls. For the artist, writer, composer or architect, whose tradition of craft is 'based on accumulated experience or continuous usage'[4] and handed down, the result may be a crucial loss of intellectual and social discourse with society. In many ways the function of the responsible artist has much in common with that of the judge for both have to make judicious and considered decisions which may affect the traditions our generation passes on. The judge acts on the law, and the artist or architect on works of art and architecture in the public realm. Both should embody and vivify, and when appropriate propose to modify, our fundamental ideals and beliefs.

Freedom and its opposites
Freedom is one of the most cherished achievements. We 'hand it down' to our children as a rare prize, yet in order to fully understand its implications, we must also study its opposites.

Whereas freedom depends upon the precise definition of bounds to create an ordered context for nurturing life, its two opposites strive to limit, subvert or destroy freedom.

The first is a state of bondage, which may involve physical, legal, political, social or religious fetters. These may be applied in many different ways to different degrees before the individual is totally enslaved. The many shades of grey between the extremes of freedom and slavery are of vital importance in defining a set of bounds. The second opposite is equally terrifying. This is a state of chaos in which choice has neither meaning nor significance as all action, all choice, is equally important and equally irrelevant. No decision is considered to have relevance beyond itself. In bondage of slavery, choice is so limited as to be ineffective. In chaos, because there is total disorder, it is meaningless! Because of the unlimited range of possibilities, we may not even be aware of our lack of freedom. Chaos and bondage are at opposite ends of a spectrum of choice – one unlimited, one too limited. Freedom becomes the fulcrum that finds the optimal point of balance between these extremes.

The Bible describes the earth before creation as 'unformed and void'. In Hebrew this phrase is *tohu v'vohu,* which means chaos. In such a state nothing has form or significance and life is not possible. Form, by its very nature, exists by virtue of bounds or limits which define its particular characteristics. The Kabbalah describes the creation told in Genesis as a process of God limiting himself in order to create the forms of our world.

Drexler understood freedom and its relation to both of its opposite states of bondage and chaos. First he associated 'freedom' with one opposite; the constrictive bonds imposed by the 'reductionist' imperative of engineering. By accepting efficiency as an operating ideal and striving to achieve most with least means, the engineer submits to the determinism of natural law. These bonds are too narrow a yoke and severely limit, indeed virtually preclude, freedom and choice. The single exercise of freedom is the initial decision to submit to this particular yoke. All subsequent decisions are reductionist and deterministic. This impacts in two different ways: *efficient design and cheap construction.* Efficiency is the goal of the engineer with specific design tasks to fulfil. The goal is to maximise ends with least means. Efficiency involves exploiting natural law by the synthesis of a clear design concept and an efficient use of materials. Such a goal is not appropriate to architecture.

Design in architecture is based on a very different set of parameters. Typically a building is an elaborate series of compromises between the often conflicting and overlapping demands of functional, efficient operation and maintenance of electrical, plumbing, security and air-conditioning equipment, construction methods, safety codes, zoning, union regulations, financing, and tax law. At a more fundamental level, the architect should satisfy the needs of various users of the building and produce a competent work of architecture. A set of construction drawings and specifications for a small building may incorporate over a million decisions. The architect is forced, continuously, to strive to find the optimal series of compromises. This is a time-consuming process and may be costly to construct. Sadly, few clients are prepared to devote either time or means to achieve good architecture. The outcome is neither efficient design nor artful compromise, but cheap construction exploiting shoddy building techniques and low-grade materials. The Modernistic architect's rallying cry, 'Less is more', turned out to be a dream come true for developers and government authorities, but quite the opposite for the public, users of buildings and connoisseurs of great architecture.

Reductivism and chaos
Whereas the engineering imperative has led architecture into a

state of bondage, the curious history of the depoliticisation of Modernistic architecture has led it to the other extreme – the chaos of unlimited choice. This transformation occurred over a period of 30 or 40 years. At the outset, in the 1920s, the Modernist architect's espousal of the 'reductionist imperatives of the engineering style' remained more an ideal than a fact. In this context it should be also considered as part of the ideological ethos of Europe of the late teens and 20s. The Russian revolution proposed that a new society be realised through the inevitable advent of scientific socialism, based on new, more efficient patterns of social, economic and political organisation. It would supplant the Europe of king, church and class which Marxists regarded as callous, corrupt, incompetent and to be largely responsible for the debacle of World War One. The emergence of the new man and the scientific new world order would render obsolete, for all time, existing economic, social and political systems together with their cities, towns and villages and related means of production. Those who advocated such a priority believed it was the task of the new architecture to reorder life in the new society by the design of new types of towns and cities. The programmes of Congrès Internationaux d'Architecture Moderne (CIAM) and Le Corbusier's *Ville Radieuse* are examples of serious and very influential proposals for a new urban order.

The theory stipulated, however, that until the advent of the revolution, this new urban and rural order could not be realised. Nevertheless, architects could point the way by the design of new buildings each of which was an advanced outpost of the new world to come. The new physical order was to be scientifically structured and value-free, as inevitable as the order of nature herself. The Modernist architects' battle cry was: 'form follows function and expresses the mode of construction'. Thus, the political revolution was accompanied by a parallel one in architecture. The architecture of past and present was simply brushed aside by the 'progressive' modes of the new 'engineering' and 'scientific' imperatives of Modernistic design and planning.

In the United States, Modernistic architecture's social and political programme was not taken very seriously. From the outset it was merely seen to be a style, called by Hitchcock and Johnson the *International Style*.[5] To an ardent believer in Modernistic architecture's revolutionary programme, this was heresy. The ideal of scientific socialism, on the one hand, and the arbitrariness implied by the idea of style – implying one among many equally valid approaches – on the other, are not compatible. The one inevitably cancels out the substance of the other.

By the late 1950s, the gradual realisation of the true extent of Stalinist oppression and of the failure of the Soviet dream discredited the revolutionary meaning that had been implicit in the new forms of Modernistic architecture. The shell of Modernism remained intact as a style, but retained only shards of its political programme. Nevertheless, application of the architectural and city planning programme of CIAM to existing cities, whose development was predicated on very different economic and social structures, carried the seeds of urban disaster.

The Modernist vision of cities: isolated, self-referential buildings set in parks, resulted in urban chaos when applied to existing cities. As it spread across five continents, blight, banal architecture and shoddy construction continued to grow in its wake on a scale not hitherto conceivable. Norman Mailer described this an an 'empty landscape of psychosis'.[6] Local custom and traditions were ignored, buildings indiscriminately levelled, and centuries of urban growth, character and development simply 'trashed'. This was a state of chaos in which all decisions appeared to be equally irrelevant, the condition to be beyond improvement, and any attempt to propose common bounds seen as abrogating freedom. P Morton Shand, an early champion of modern design, eloquently outlined this nightmare in a letter written just prior to his death, to Sir John Betjeman:

> I have frightul nightmares, and no wonder, for I am haunted by a gnawing sense of guilt in having, in however minor and obscure degree, helped bring about, anyhow encouraged and praised, the embryo searchings that have now materialised into a monster neither of us could have foreseen: Contemporary Architecture (the piling up of gigantic children's toy bricks in utterly dehumanised and meaningless forms), 'Art' and all that. It is no longer funny: it is a frightening, all pervading menace.[7]

Devoid of its socialist base, CIAM's search for a new and objective urban order to use as the basis for new development was then replaced by a series of individual architect's proposals for a new urban order. Under this new ethos a premium was placed on the untrammelled, inventive ingenuity of the individual architect. Here is a paradox: an architectural ideology based on scientific socialism proposing an objective and unified vision of architecture and urbanism culminates in liberating the ego of the individual architect giving it unfettered license to reorganise and revolutionise the urban environment. The literature of the period 1950-1980 is filled with grandiose proposals by individual architects for reordering cities. The architectural chaos that followed is evident in the incoherent piecemeal appearance of most new urban and suburban development.

Today our response remains incoherent and inconsequential. We attempt to preserve buildings of the past for future generations but are unable to produce a cogent and coherent vision of the future of architecture and urbanism. The failure of architecture to fulfil obligations that society has taken for granted for three millenia has become an accepted feature of practice and education. We appear to have lost all hope of creating a sense of order, diversity, harmony and beauty by using physical planning to coordinate activity in architecture, landscape architecture and urban design as architects, clients and developers did in the past. Modernistic architecture's major legacy is threefold: urban chaos; the unsurpassed banality of most architecture and building of the past four decades; and intellectual collapse and loss of hope in architecture's ability to solve real human and social problems and a few isolated architectural masterpieces, typically freestanding suburban houses, by Le Corbusier, Mies van der Rohe and others.

An alternative vision

This is the context in which Arthur Drexler posited 'freedom', with the options of alternative visions, ideas and points of view, as a 'necessity' because it offered possible ways out of the straightjacket of Modernism's reductivist design and CIAM's city planning. The exhibition of student work from the Ecole was a way of starting to formulate an alternative to the present. The exhibition displayed the exquisite renderings by students of their design projects, but its major thrust was presenting the Ecole's system of education.

Drexler did not want to substitute Modernism's tired platitudes with another series of 'isms'. To this end, he presented a system of education which encouraged scholarship, facilitated asking difficult questions, and allowed for pursuit and exploration of answers. Implicit in the exhibition were two key questions. *First* was the question of methodology or how to approach architectural design. The focus was on one particular approach from the past but Drexler's major concern was architectural practice today, and in the future, in the climate of political freedom and economic opportunity which was an outcome of World War Two. It posed this problem: if political, religious and personal freedom is an essential component of life, could Modernism be adapted to reflect this new ethos of choice? If not, what is the most fruitful approach to reformulation of architectural education to solve problems of design and urbanism?

The *second* question deals with the relationship of methodology of design and the resultant architecture it produced. The exhibition examined a few examples from the corpus of architecture and urban design work produced by some of the most important graduates of the Ecole des Beaux-Arts. This consisted of examples of 19th-century French architecture, supplemented by the work of a few American graduates in the United States. The exhibition forced architects and historians to look at and seriously study a major body of work which has been ignored by most architectural historians. For Drexler the validity of a design methodology depends on the architecture and urbanism it produces.

To exercise freedom, Drexler stressed the need for an architectural context in which 'freedom' has relevance. This mandates defining a set of bounds to focus creative energy in directions that are fruitful and positive for society. As a model Drexler suggested we look at how students at the Ecole were taught to approach design for over 200 years, which in turn provides a springboard for the study of how architects have approached design for 3,000 years prior to 1920. With such knowledge in hand, we are able to compare and reassess Modernistic architecture's design methods.

Imitation

Imitation was the method to approach design most used by architects of ancient Greece and Rome, the Byzantine and Gothic periods, and the Renaissance. It was formalised into a rigorous programme of study at the Ecole. The process of *imitation* was a means to confront and discourse with the past in order to assimilate and transform it according to present needs. This occurred at a variety of levels.

First, imitation is similar to the case study method used in law. It is a process by which various solutions to a similar type of problem, or set of problems, are examined in order to determine the optimal approach to a particular project. For example, at the Ecole, the system of room arrangement by which a building plan was organised was called a *parti*. Precedents for *partis* were collected from the work of great architects of the past as well as from student entries for the school's many formal competitions. These competitions were so important that they formed the basis of the design curriculum. Students also visited Italy, and later Greece, to study ancient and Renaissance buildings. Their measured drawings and renderings of these buildings were collected in the great standard reference works of D'Espouy, Letarouilly, and others which are still in use today. The practice of student study abroad followed the example of the great Renaissance architects who journeyed to Rome to sketch and measure the ruins of ancient Rome at first hand. Andrea Palladio, for example, included his measured drawings of ancient Roman buildings and decorative details in his *Four Books of Architecture* of 1570, which remains one of the most influential and enduring handbooks on architecture ever published. Antoine Desgodetz compared drawings of ancient buildings by Palladio and other architects with his own accurate measurements in order to determine how they used precedent.[8]

The Ecole de Beaux-Arts' use of imitation was very similar to the case study method instituted by Christopher Columbus Langdell as the basis of the curriculum at the Harvard Law School just over a century ago. Both curricula worked from precedent to establish a rational basis for the development of strategies to solve problems.

In architecture, the close examination of previous buildings of a similar type yields solutions to both aesthetic and functional problems. Rejection, acceptance or modification of norms as well as experimentation and innovation could be calculated and controlled by comparison with precedents. Imitation facilitates and promotes analysis of function in various building types. Such diverse issues as administration, public policy, building and health codes are assessed by comparison of completed buildings, synthesised into a precise and comprehensive programme of accommodation, and finally translated into spatial relationships within the proposed building. The approximate 'bubble diagram' method still favoured by Modernists is claimed to be 'value free'; does not rely on past examples; and is too limited in scope to be tested or evaluated. These bubble diagrams reduce a building to sets of undifferentiated spatial relationships connected by lines. A line connecting two bubbles may imply a door or passage between two discrete rooms, a partition between two separate spaces in one room, a glass partition, or merely two groupings of furniture on either side of an aisle. As a technique it is all but useless for serious study. It does, however, leave much to the judgement of the architect that cannot be verified and is seldom even discussed with the client. Modernism still eschews contact with the past, considering it irrelevant, and regards its own history as the only history worth studying. Imitation on the other hand is structured to engage the past in an active dialogue.

The practising architect uses the same principle of imitation employed by the student but more comprehensively. The stage of mastering the basics of grammar and syntax is replaced by more serious concerns about function, site, construction and aesthetics – the manipulation of form to embody meaning and create beauty. The architect engages tradition first by ingesting and assimilating a complex vocabulary and literature of architecture. This corpus becomes so integrated into the architect's mind and memory that it informs his every creative gesture. The tradition itself may be seen as a building on which the architect improves and expands. For the Renaissance artist or architect, to imitate was 'to act freely, to select and . . . to retain a sense of oneself.'[9]

The architect was measured by the quality of the sources he or she chose to examine and incorporate into the process of designing a building. Assimilating a great work or a series of masterpieces was infinitely more difficult than using minor buildings. By scholarly consideration of precedent, both of form, function and construction, an architect could 'surpass the past while using forms the past could give him.'[10] In this vein, Aretino wrote of Giulio Romano as 'anciently modern and modernly ancient.'[11] Sir Edwin Lutyens eloquently described the process of imitation in a letter to Herbert Baker. Writing about the design of Heathcote, he expressed a moving reverence for the orders and a deep, intuitive understanding of the work methodology of his great Greek and Italian predecessors:

That time worn Doric Order – a lovely thing – I have the cheek to adopt. You can't copy it. To be right you have to take it and design it. You, as an exercise, take the order out of a book, as it stands, and couple the columns . . . see what happens? Your bases interlock! Inigo Jones solved the difficulty in one way and very good. Vanbrugh failed lamentably and clumsily, Wren avoided the problem. The problem is to get the two posts, with their triglyphs and metopes complete, proper in all parts, and let the bases interlock and without distortion of their bases, and then the soffits of the stones and their digested completeness. You cannot copy: you find if you do you are caught, a mess remains. It means hard labour, hard thinking, over every line in all three dimensions and in every joint; and no stone can be allowed to slide. If you tackle it in this way, the Order belongs to you, and every stroke, being mentally handled, must become endowed with such poetry and artistry as God has given you.[12]

Engaging the past

The architect engages in both a dialogue and a competition with the past. When Lutyens described the struggle to resolve an age-old design problem involving pairing of Doric columns, he focused on form. Picasso, on the other hand, spoke of meaning when he describes 'imitating' the 'magic' of primitive art.[13]

For a master, imitation was and still is an engagement with tradition itself and an opportunity to expand, redefine, extend or illuminate a part of it. Even the best work of great Modernists like Frank Lloyd Wright, Le Corbusier and Mies van der Rohe, which consistently used the *inversion* of traditional ideas and forms, operated with reference to the canon of Classical architects.[14] This recognition of tradition, albeit perversely, is a quality that differentiated their work from that of their peers and successors for whom history was irrelevant.

The principle of imitation enabled the great masters of the past to weave the marvellous, rich tapestry of Classical and Gothic architectural history. 20th-century masterpieces like the Memorial Arch at Thiepval (1927-32) by Sir Edwin Lutyens, the old Pennsylvania Railroad Terminal, New York (1902-11) by McKim Mead & White, now sadly demolished, and the Empire State Building (1931) by Shreve, Lamb & Harmon are testimony to the continuing vitality of *imitation* in this century as a design methodology.

Imitation, or working from precedent, was seen as a decisive advantage, for it enabled architect and client to absorb all the experience of the past. The method identified various building types, like churches, courthouses or hospitals, each of which had similarities irrespective of its location. Imitation focused on what a particular building type may have had in common with past efforts making it easier for the architect and client to isolate and deal with the unique and special features of their project. Anyone designing a house, skyscraper or even a detail had to compare and evaluate the new design with the accumulated experience of the past. By utilising typological solutions to solve formal and functional design problems, the architect was *freed* to refine, perfect and elaborate a particular solution. Informed rejection was also an option, but only, of course, after due consideration. Without a norm there could be neither innovation nor measured and calculated development. In the past, these design paradigms were public knowledge and encompassed both commodity, firmness and delight.[15] They incorporated current social, organisational and architectural norms and in this way it was relatively easy to adapt solutions to each client's need and taste, to facilitate participation by users of the building in the preparation of design and programme (about which so much is said today and so little done), and to evaluate both aesthetic and functional innovations.

We have misunderstood, indeed forgotten, the distinction Renaissance artists and architects made between the acts of *copying* and *imitating*. To *copy* was 'to lose dignity, to act unfreely.'[16] It was to parrot the past by using its forms literally and therefore without understanding. To copy is absurd for the past cannot be repeated. The different details of each new architectural problem, whether of site, programme, construction technique or aesthetic expression mandates individual solution and expression. To ape someone else's solution is like trying to palm off one person's portrait as that of another, a pitfall well described by Francesco Petrarca:

> He who imitates must have a care that what he writes be similar, not identical [with his model], and that the similarity should not be of the kind that obtains between a portrait and a sitter, where the artist earns the more praise the greater the likeness, but rather of the kind that obtains between a son and his father. Here, though there may often be a great difference between their individual features, a

certain shadow and, as our painters call it, air perceptible above all in the face and eyes produces that similarity that reminds us of the father as soon as we see the son, even though if the matter were put to measurement all parts would be found to be different; some hidden quality there has this power. So we too should take care that when one thing is like, many should be unlike, and that what is like should be hidden so as to be grasped only by the mind's silent enquiry, intelligible rather than describable. We should therefore make use of another man's inner quality and tone, but avoid his words. For the one kind of similarity is hidden and the other protrudes; the one creates poets, the other apes.[17]

The work of architects in the past was as personal as those of architects today and more urbane and functional. The hand of a Hawksmoor, Bramante, Sansavino or Lutyens can be detected in a single cornice or niche. The principle of *imitation* allowed the genius to follow in the footsteps of the masters and expand inherited tradition by subtle innovation. How else can one account for the brilliant development of the Gothic vault and pier, or the dazzling perfection of individual works like Michelangelo's Capitoline Hill, Hawksmoor's Christ Church, Spitalfields, or Mansart's Château Longeuil at Maison-sur-Seine? The less-gifted architect could use tradition to create individual works of superb competence, as well as urbane groups of buildings, whose total impact transcends the quality of the individual structures as illustrated by the extraordinary general quality and urbanity of 18th-century English and French architecture and design.

Imitation and assimilation

This process of imitation was aptly summarised by Sir Joshua Reynolds in his Discourse VI:

> Invention, strictly speaking, is little more than a new combination of those images which have been previously gathered and deposited in the memory; nothing can come of nothing: he who has laid up no materials can produce no combinations. A student unacquainted with the attempts of former adventurers is always apt to overrate his own abilities; to mistake the most trifling excursions for discoveries of moment, and every coast new to him for a new-found country. If by chance he passes beyond his usual limits, he congratulates his own arrival at those regions which they who have steered a better course have long left behind them ... if we were forbid to make use of the advantages which our predecessors afford us, the art would be always to begin, and consequently remain always in its infant state; and it is a common observation, that no art was ever invented and carried to perfection at the same time. I am ... pursuaded that by imitation only, variety, and even originality of invention, is produced. What is learnt from others becomes really our own, sinks deep, and is never forgotten, nay, it is by seizing on this clue that we proceed forward, and get further and further in enlarging the principles and improving the practice of our art. Study, therefore, the great works of the great masters forever. Study ... those masters ... consider them as models which are to imitate and at the same time as rivals with whom you are to contend.[18]

Imitation culminates in assimilation. Critics like Blake, for example, who claimed that taste and genius are born with us and cannot be acquired, confused imitation with its end: *assimilation*. This is the process by which in Reynolds' words, 'what is learnt from others, becomes really our own'. The difference between competent, often undistinguished buildings, background buildings (which have always made up the vast bulk of urban construction) and the masterpiece is in the degree of assimilation. The process by which a Michelangelo or Hawksmoor assimilates and focuses the vast store of knowledge and experience to create the masterpiece remains a mystery. To this extent we may concur with Blake. That they used the process of imitation as a starting point is beyond dispute. Furthermore, one aspect of a masterpiece is the unique integration of tradition with a particular time and place by a unique individual.

Imitation then also functions as a means by which norms are passed from one generation to the next and adjusted to present needs. It is a way of expanding tradition by engagement with the past. Drexler wondered whether the method of imitation could be used within the Modernist tradition to expand the choices available to the architect in an era of unparalleled political freedom. We do have a few great works in the Modernist idiom that integrate into the canon by drawing on precedent, albeit by inversion. But imitation is so integral to the language of Classical architecture that it cannot be plucked from its place without bringing the entire Classical tradition with it.

In the first place this occurs because Modernist architecture, by its own assertion, wants to start from zero, whereas imitation creates a dialogue with precedent and the past. Second, evolution of Modernist architecture since 1945 has led to a cast of individualist 'geniuses', each more anxious than the next to make a unique signature across our cityscape. Disdain and disregard for a client's wishes and needs and the character of the surrounding city typify this ego-centred architecture. In contradistinction, imitation promotes the value of buildings integrating into a pre-existing city, with all the challenges and limitations this implies, and fosters a strong, respectful architect-client relationship. Furthermore it offers a common language to client and architect which Modernism eschews and simply hasn't had time to develop even if it wanted to.

Third, creativity depends on tradition. It requires a complex language with a rich literature that delicately balances stability and flexibility. A living organism needs both skeleton and softer tissue. The immense variety of Classical architecture was created in response to the needs of diverse societies with their particular cultures, religions, geographies, climates and environments. The architectural traditions of Spain, France, Italy, England and Russia, for example, each constitute a specific tradition with its own associations, meanings, formal characteristics and history. The extraordinary range and brilliance of Classical architecture testifies to the flexibility of the Classical architectural tradition. The creative powers of the human mind can be fully engaged only within such a vast tradition. This architectural virtuosity flourished and persisted because the vocabulary and canons of Classical architecture are a set of bounds within which the artist may exercise freedom in the service of enhancing life.

Fourth, imitation engages the architect in the vast wealth of the Classical tradition. This dialogue with the past is invaluable for the creation of new work that integrates into the tradition. Architecture, more than any other art, requires this integration for we see the cumulative work of centuries in one glance in our great cities. The present must relate to the past for cities to grow in a healthy, harmonious and orderly fashion. Our notion of the city, its organisation, the hierarchy and meaning of its form is Classical. The city cannot grow without the very buildings to which the new ones must relate, without referring to precedent, without imitating. Thus Modernism abdicates its responsibility to the city as a living organism unless it integrates precedent and yet, this act would mean abdicating the reductionist values and ethos of personal expression that reign today. If Modernism chose to learn from imitation, it would modify itself so that it is no longer what we call Modernism. It would begin to integrate into itself the wisdom of the Classical tradition.

The time is surely ripe for us in England and the United States to look again at the magnificent architectural tradition of the West and to reassess the direction of our architecture. Expanding our concept and view of 20th-century architecture reveals that the continuity of Classical and Gothic architecture has never really been broken. This point can be made graphically, by an architectural time-line from 1000 BC-1979 AD, from ancient Greece to the present, on which Modernistic architecture occupies about one-half inch of a 30-inch-long line. The true challenge of the future is once again to master our great architectural tradition and through the medium of imitation and assimilation, to interpret it according to the needs of our time.

Notes

1 Arthur Drexler, 'Engineer's Architecture: Truth and Its Consequences', *The Architecture of the Ecole des Beaux-Arts*, Museum of Modern Art, New York, 1977, p15.

2 *Concise Oxford English Dictionary*, Oxford University Press, Oxford, 1985, p 1135, 21.

3 I M Bunim, *Ethics From Sinai*, Philip Feldheim, New York, 1964, p 26.

4 *Concise Oxford English Dictionary, op cit*, p 1135, 3.

5 Henry-Russell Hitchcock and Philip Johnson, The *International Style*, New York, 1932.

6 Norman Mailer, 'Mailer versus Scully', *Architectural Forum*, April 1964, p 97.

7 John Betjeman, 'P Morton Shand', *Architectural Review*, November 1960, p 327.

8 Hector d'Espouy, ed, *Fragments d'Architecture Antique*, 2 vols, Paris, 1905; Paul M Letarouilly, *Edifices de Rome Moderne*, 3 vols, Paris, 1840-57; Andrea Palladio, *The Four Books of Architecture*, trans Isaac Ware 1738, Dover Publications, New York, 1965; and Antoine Desgodetz, *Les Edifices Antiques de Rome*, Paris, 1682.

9 David Cast, 'Liberty: Honor: Virtue: Comment on the Position of the Visual Arts in the Renaissance', *Yale Italian Studies*, Fall 1977, p 375.

10 *ibid*.

11 Pietro Arentino, *Il secondo libro delle lettere*, ed F Nicolini Bari, 1916, in E H Gombrich, *Norm and Form*, Phaidon, Oxford, 1977, p127.

12 Francis Pollen, 'The Last of the Classicists', *Country Life*, April 3 1969, p 375.

13 Francesco Pellizzi, 'Adventures of the Symbol: Magic for the Sake of Art', *Lectures on Constructed Thought*, The Cooper Union for the Advancement of Science and Art, 1986, p 3.

14 Allan Greenberg, 'Lutyens' Architecture Restudied', *Perspecta 12, The Yale Architectural Journal*, 1969, pp 129-152.

15 Allan Greenberg, 'Design Methodology in the 18th and 20th Centuries, VIA III, Ornament, Journal of the Graduate School of Fine Arts*, University of Pennsylvania, pp 65-82; and John Summerson, 'The Classical Country House in 18th-Century England', *Journal of the Royal Society of Arts*, July 1959, No 5036, vol CVII, pp 539-86.

16 Cast, *op cit*.

17 Francesco Petrarca, *Le familiari*, XXIII, 19, 78-94, quoted in E H Gombrich, *The Style all'antica: Imitation and Assimilation, Norm and Form*, Chicago, 1985, p122.

18 Sir Joshua Reynolds, *Discourses to the Students of the Royal Academy*, 1769-1774, ed Robert Wark, Yale University Press, New Haven, 1975, pp 93-113.

————— * —————

ALLAN GREENBERG, CONNECTICUT FARMHOUSE. *ABOVE:* LATERAL ARCADE. *BELOW:* LIBRARY

ENTRANCE

CENTRAL STAIR HALL

ALLAN GREENBERG
Farmhouse in Connecticut

SIDE PAVILION

The overall character of the house was based on Washington's Mount Vernon with its curved arcades and dependencies. The facade is faced in wood cut to look like stone, as was used in many large colonial buildings to help control the scale of the house. The entrance facade forms the central focus of a three-sided courtyard. Its pediment is held on oversized brackets, the use of the Ionic order for the front door expresses the relative importance of this entrance, as opposed to the more rustic Doric and Tuscan orders used elsewhere, and the large arched window expresses the central hall plan inside.

This facade has a strong horizontal emphasis, the width of the house being accentuated by the narrowness of the central door, arched window and bull's-eye window element in contrast to the pairs of shuttered ground-floor windows. On either side of the symmetrically composed main block are two side wings, connected by curving arcades, one housing garage and service functions, the other swimming-pool house – a large, simple space with barrel-vaulted interior and triple-sash windows. The geometry of the entrance court is further emphasised by two rows of trimmed linden trees.

The two-storey portico of the garden elevation is the focus of a long vista from the terraced gardens, a device traditional in farmhouse vernacular. Its giant paired Tuscan columns support a larger than usual span and suggest the utilitarian character of the farmhouse.

Inside the hall space with its impressive open stairwell extends through the full width of the house. An oversized broken-pedimented doorway frames a view out to the gardens. The arched window of the stair-landing in elaborate panelled casing with projecting keystone is framed by pilasters, a motif from 18th-century New England architecture.

Much attention has been paid to the high quality of detailing, with subtle variations in door pediments, cornicing, and fire mantels to suggest hierarchy in the different rooms. Although the house appears to be essentially a rarefied, academic imitation of 18th-century Palladianism, there are also small developments in the details, such as the use of additional, diagonal brackets to carry the cornicing smoothly round corners. The largest room is the library with its panelled cabinet work, whilst the more-domestic family room has warm-coloured cherry panelling on one wall only with a simple fireplace and plain cornicing, door frame and dado in the same wood.

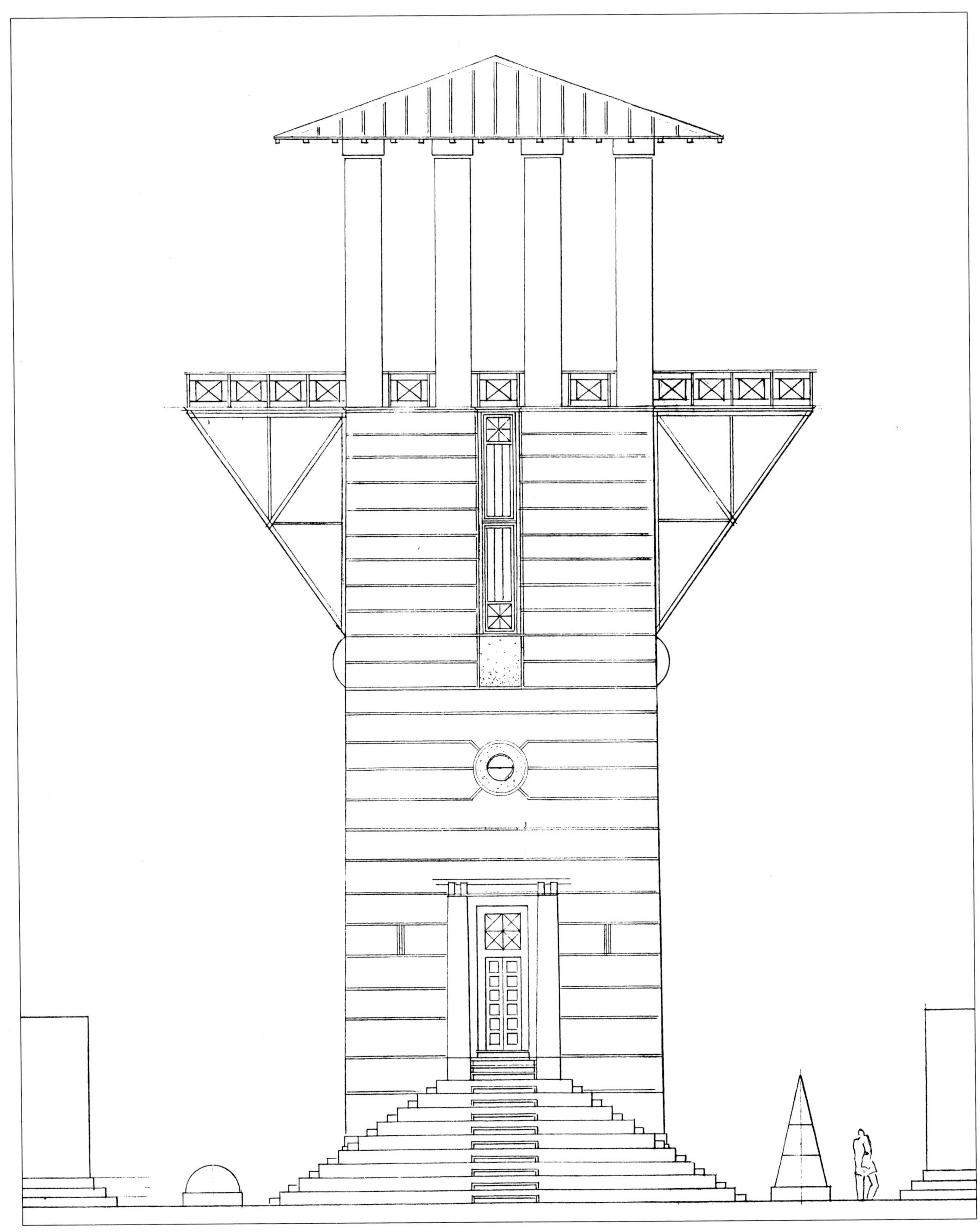

SOUTH ELEVATION

LEON KRIER
Projects in Florida and Amiens

'*Architecture is the intellectual culture of Building . . . it is concerned with the imitation and translation of the elements of building into symbolic language, expressing in a fixed system of symbols and analogies the very origin of Architecture in the laws of nature and in human intelligence and labour.*' (Leon Krier)

This tower is to be built in Seaside Florida, Duany and Plater-Zyberk's popular and successful demonstration of the imitation of traditional cities and buildings (to which Leon Krier was consultant). The tower is the very monument and keystone of the urban organisation, a centre where the city seems to converge and to begin: a place which articulates most significantly the city with its form, hierarchy, centre and boundaries and its spectacular relationship to the seaside.

This is another demonstration by Krier of the '*méthode architecturale*'. The tower (a traditional load-bearing construction in coral-stone with balconies in bronze) is a complex and elaborate invention whereby the nature of architecture is comprehensively explored without perverting the typological clarity of the building. The relationship between building and architecture, private and public, art and architecture, city and landscape, functionalism and symbolism, as well as the spatial, visual and kinesthetic experiences offered are extremely refined, complex and elegant. *Lucien Steil*

Seaside Tower

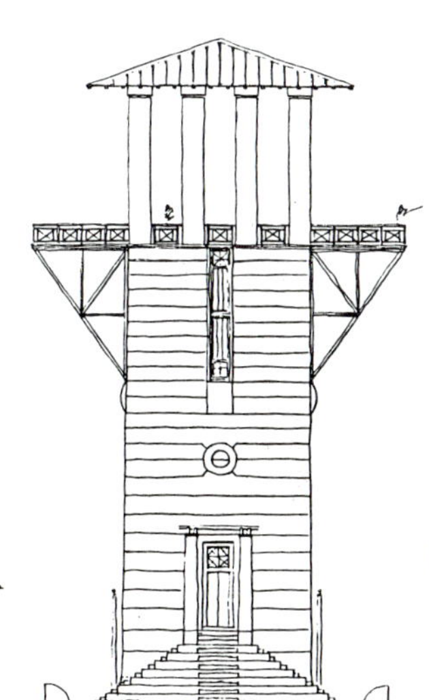

ABOVE: VIEW FROM SOUTHWEST; *BELOW*: SOUTH ELEVATION WITH LATERAL COLONNADES

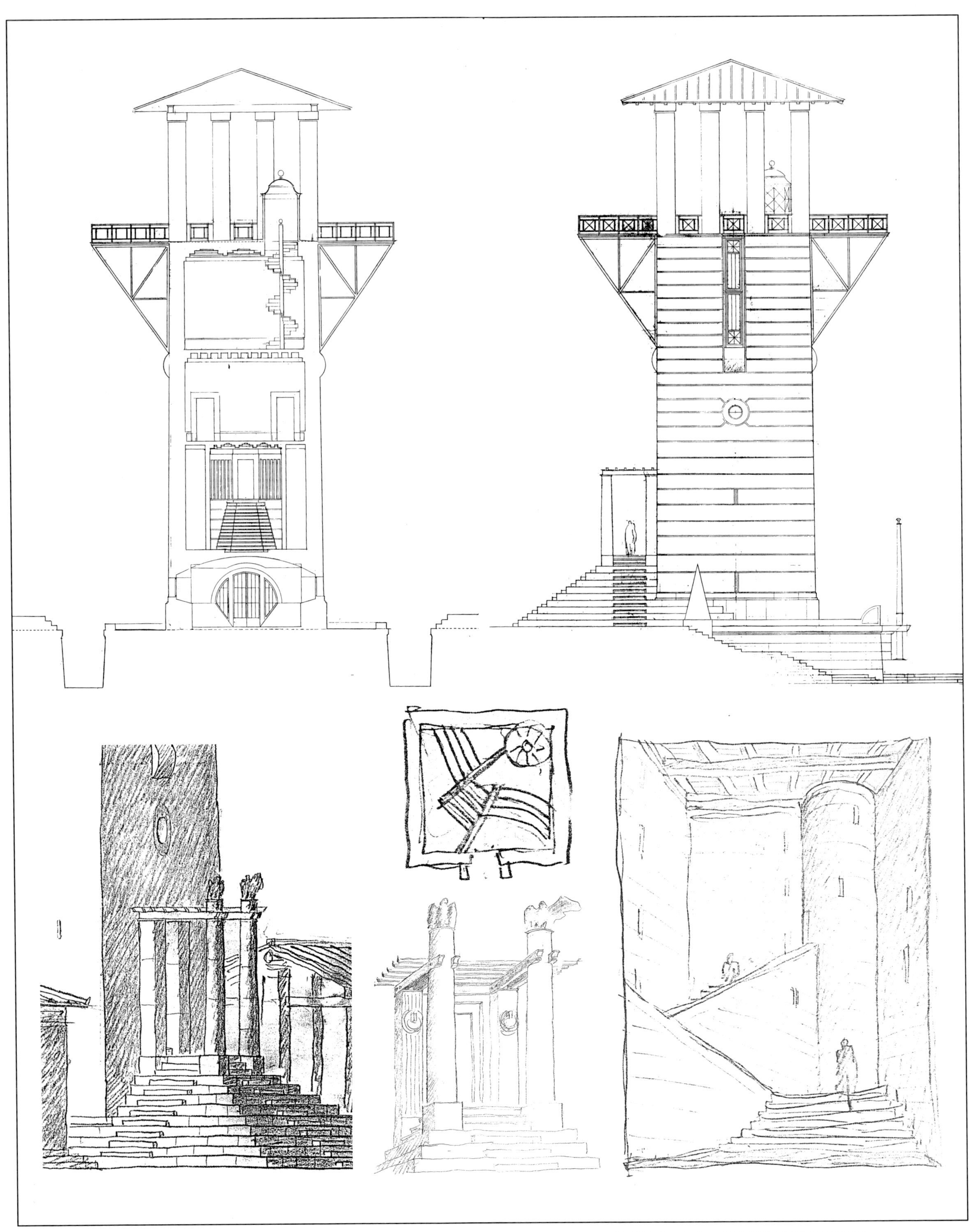

ABOVE L TO R: EAST-WEST SECTION; EAST ELEVATION. *CENTRE*: ENTRANCE HALL PLAN; *BELOW L TO R*: VIEWS OF ENTRANCE TO TOWER

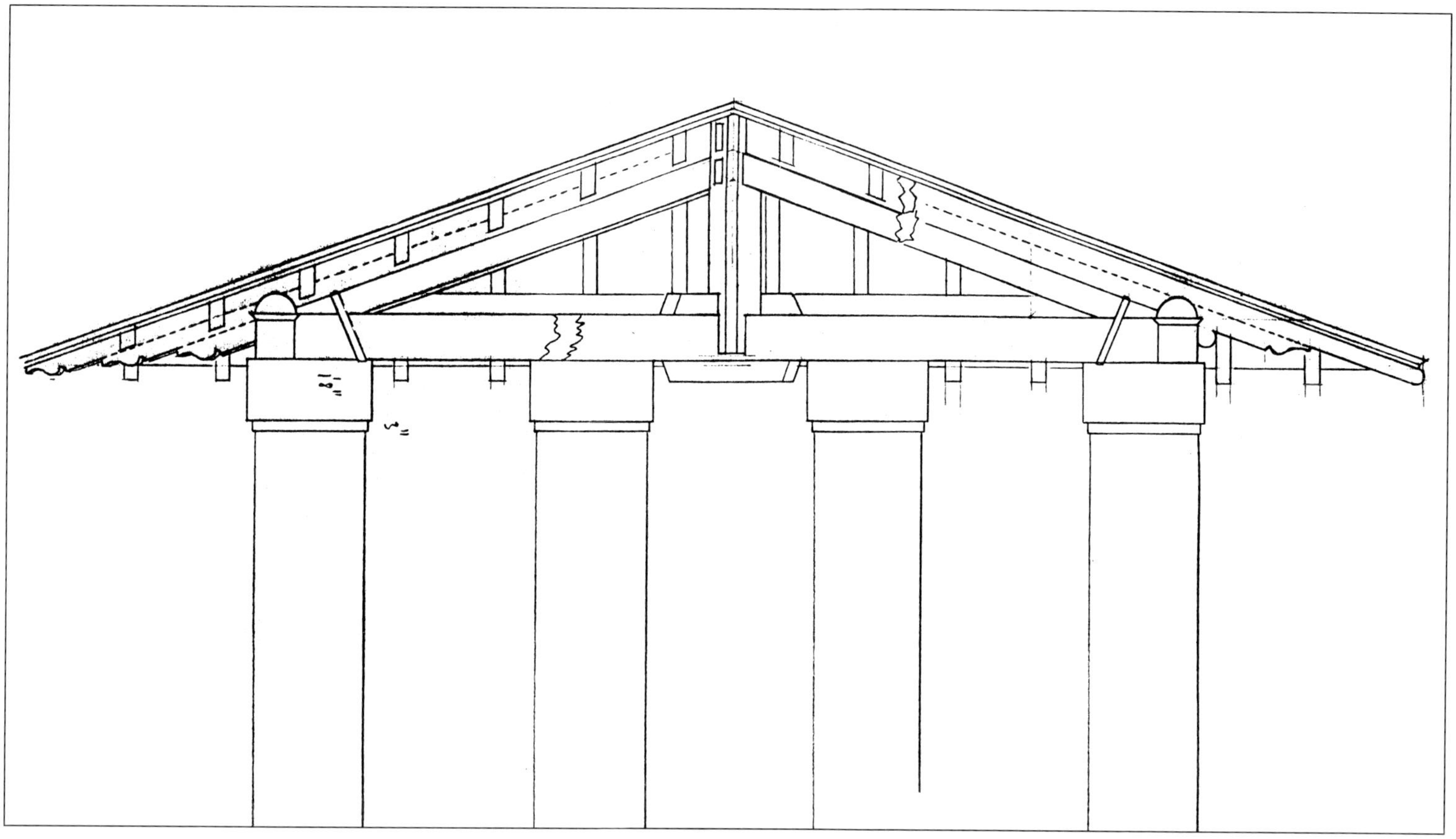

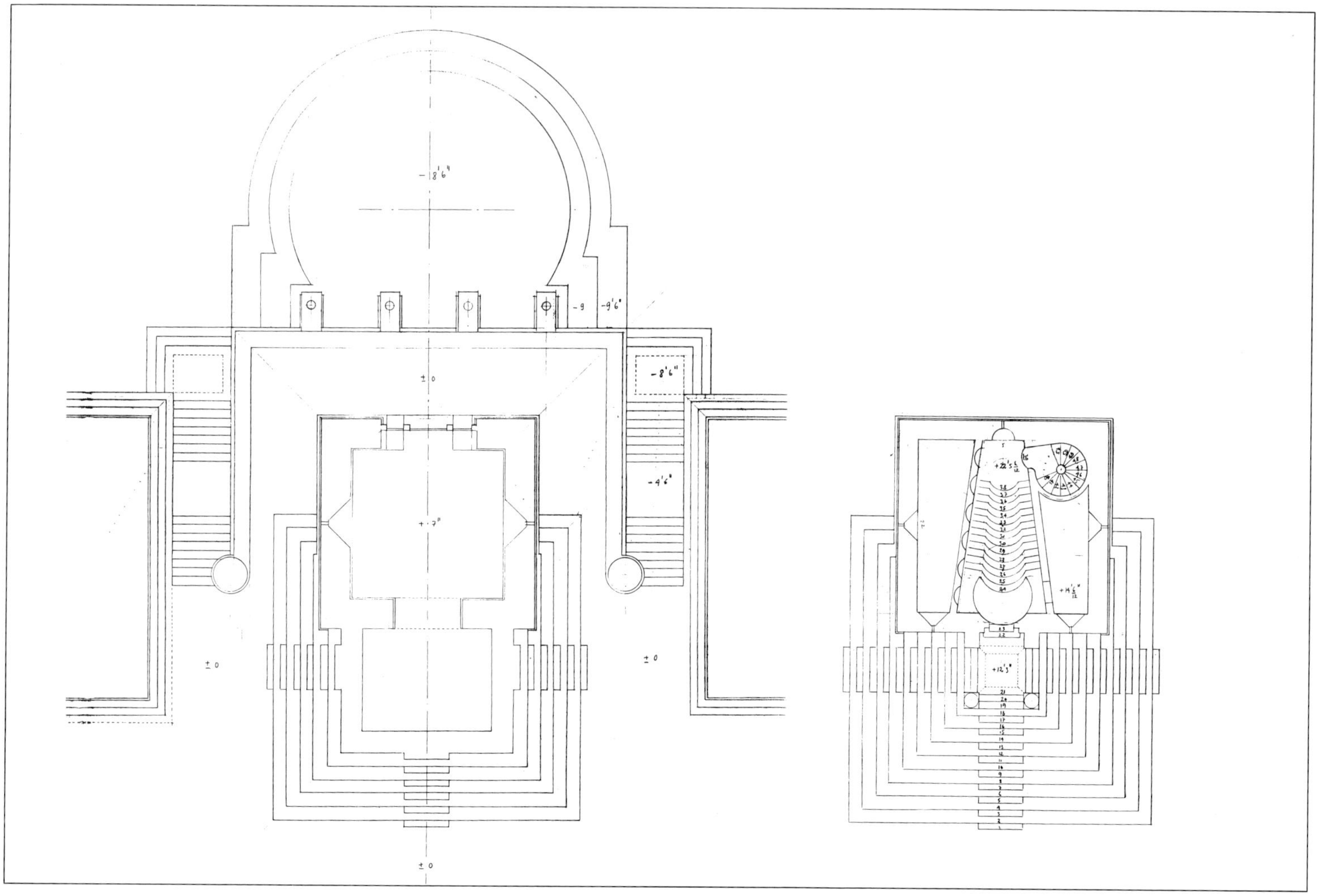

ABOVE: DETAIL OF ROOF STRUCTURE; *BELOW L TO R*: GROUND-FLOOR PLAN; 1ST-FLOOR PLAN

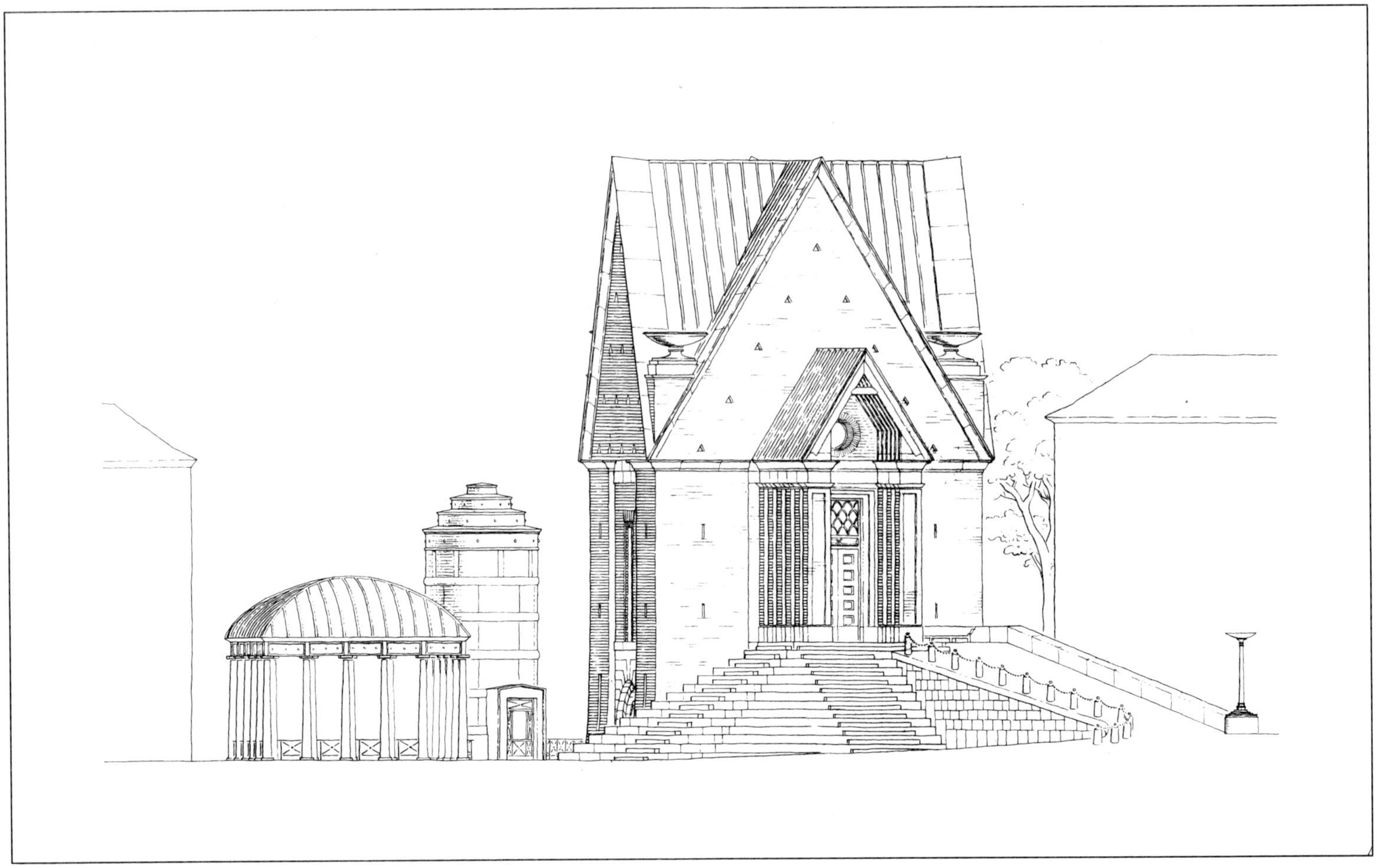

ABOVE: VIEW FROM PLACE DE L'ARCHEVECHE; BELOW: VIEW OVER CANAL

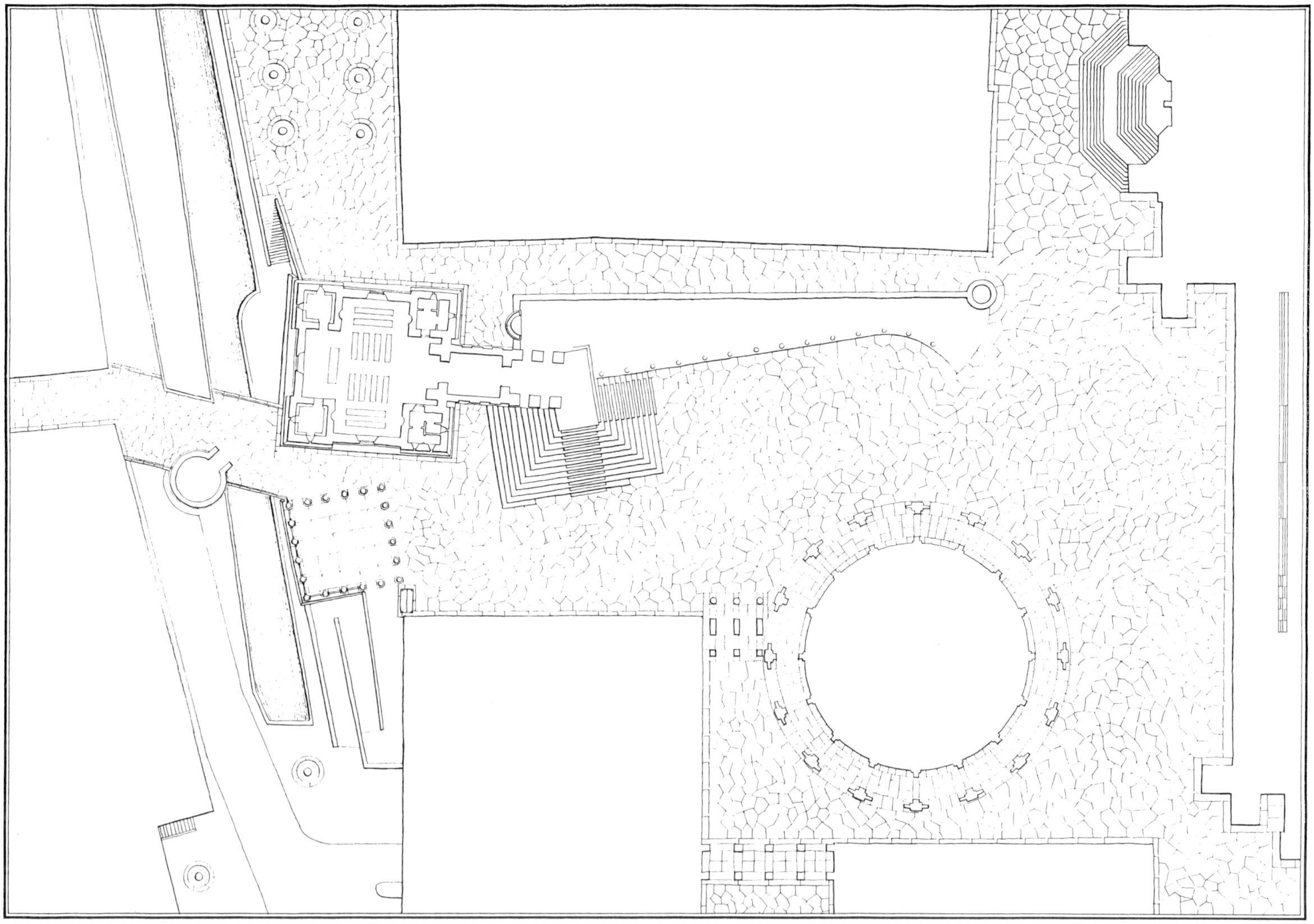

SITE PLAN

The Hall of Marriages

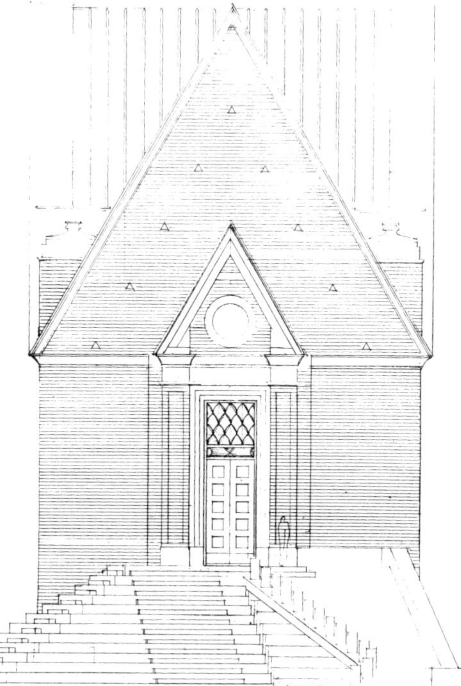

EAST FACADE WITH ENTRANCE PORTICO

Both this project and the one on page 57 were realised within the framework of the reconstruction of the historic centre of Amiens, based on a masterplan by Robert Krier.

The new Hall of Marriages is situated on the north side of the cathedral in the place de l'ancien Archevêché at the axis of important sight lines.

On the ground floor of the building, which is square in plan, there is a brasserie. This overhangs the canal with fine views of some woods to the east, while to the west its terraces extend underneath a hexastyle pavilion which together with the Hall Building forms a bridgehead between the rue de la Passerelle and the place de l'Archevêché.

The Hall is on the piano nobile. It is entered through a portico which you reach by going up a grand staircase or a ramp which occupies the whole length of the square. The roof is a wooden joist structure. The four corner pavilions contain the services, cloakroom, administration and archives. The walls, vaults, stairs and pillars are made of rough ashlar and brick, while the roof-casing and vases on the acroters are of lead. The volume of the pavilion is 14 x 14 x 25m.

Assistant: Liam O'Connor

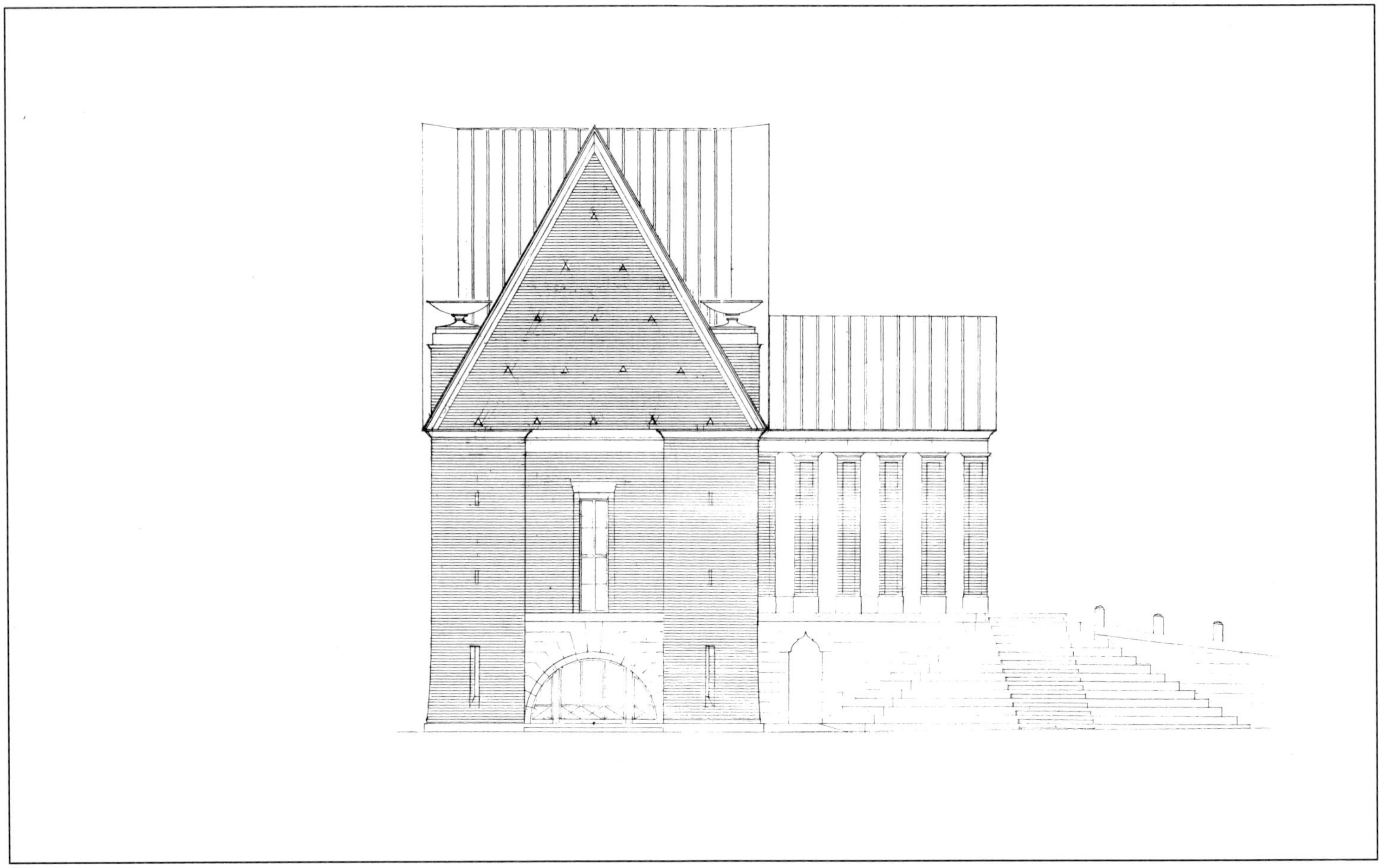

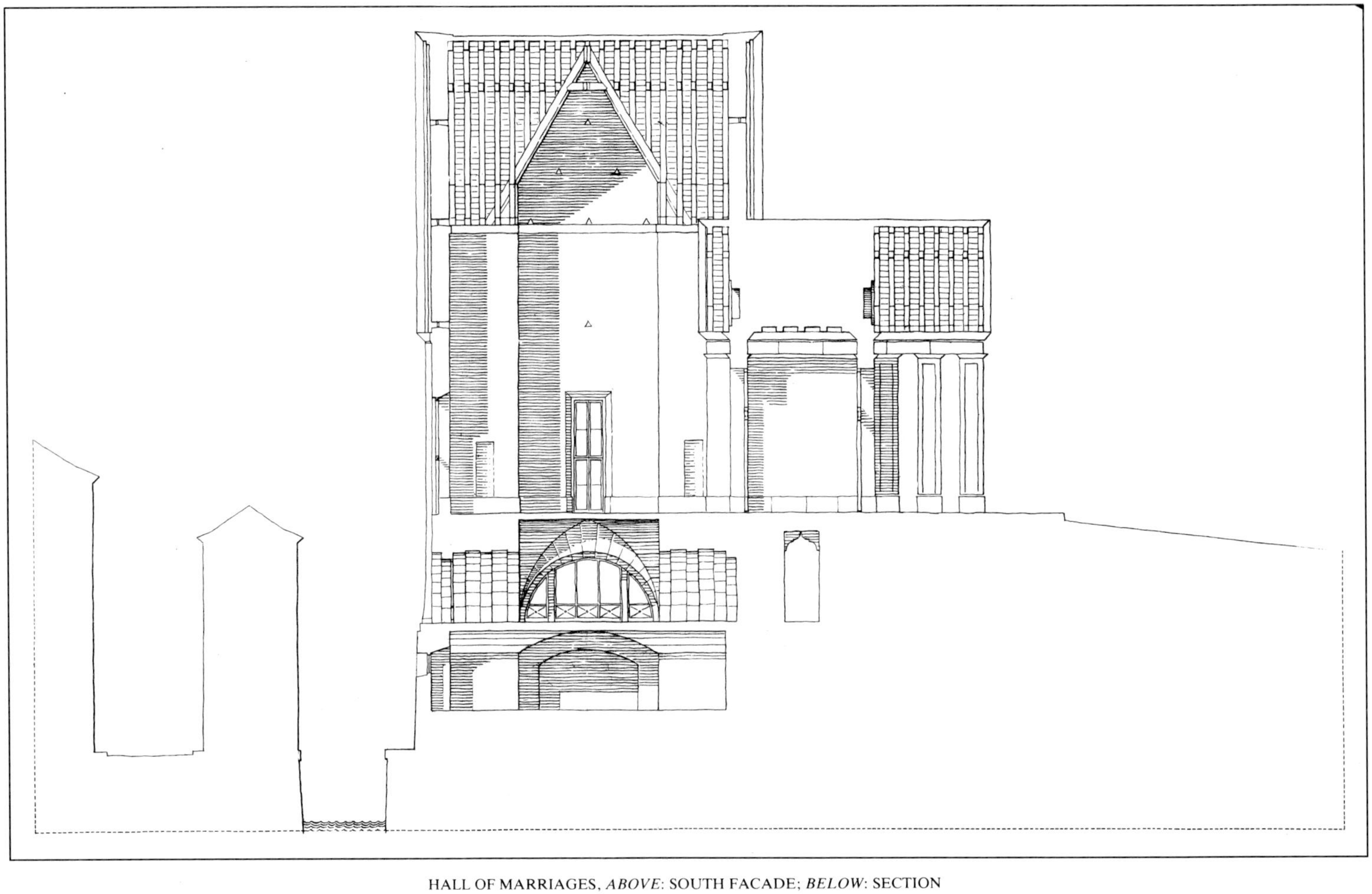

HALL OF MARRIAGES, *ABOVE*: SOUTH FACADE; *BELOW*: SECTION

SLAUGHTERHOUSE PYRAMID, *L TO R*: VIEW; SECTION

The Slaughterhouse Pyramid

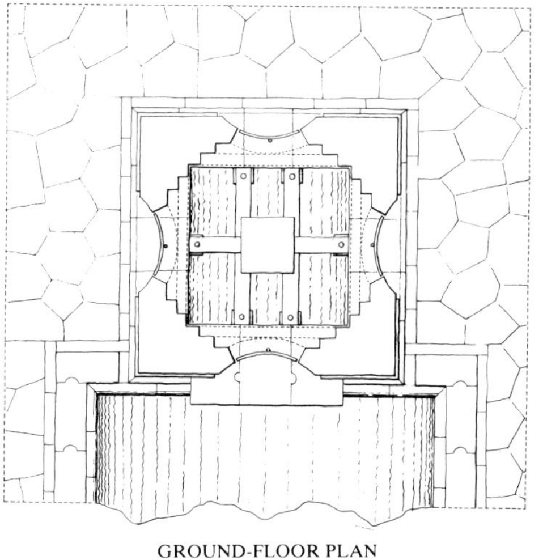

GROUND-FLOOR PLAN

This monument marks the site of an abattoir for cattle on the place de la Tuerie. It straddles the Canal de la rue basse des Tanneurs with two stone arches carrying a 5 x 5 x 5m tetrapyle. Above this is the pyramid itself, which stands 12m high and is of timber covered with copper. Its arrises (drawn from the decagon) slope at 72°. The four openings in the monument are in the form of niches protected by bronze grills. Inside they have sharply profiled architraves that are roughly cut in the grotesque manner. Looking through the openings, you see a *cella* without a floor. In the centre, suspended above the waters of the canal on three crossed oak beams, is a butcher's block, its surface marked and deformed by countless blows from the axe and knife.

Assistant: Liam O'Connor

LEON KRIER & RITA WOLFF
A Promenade in Luxembourg

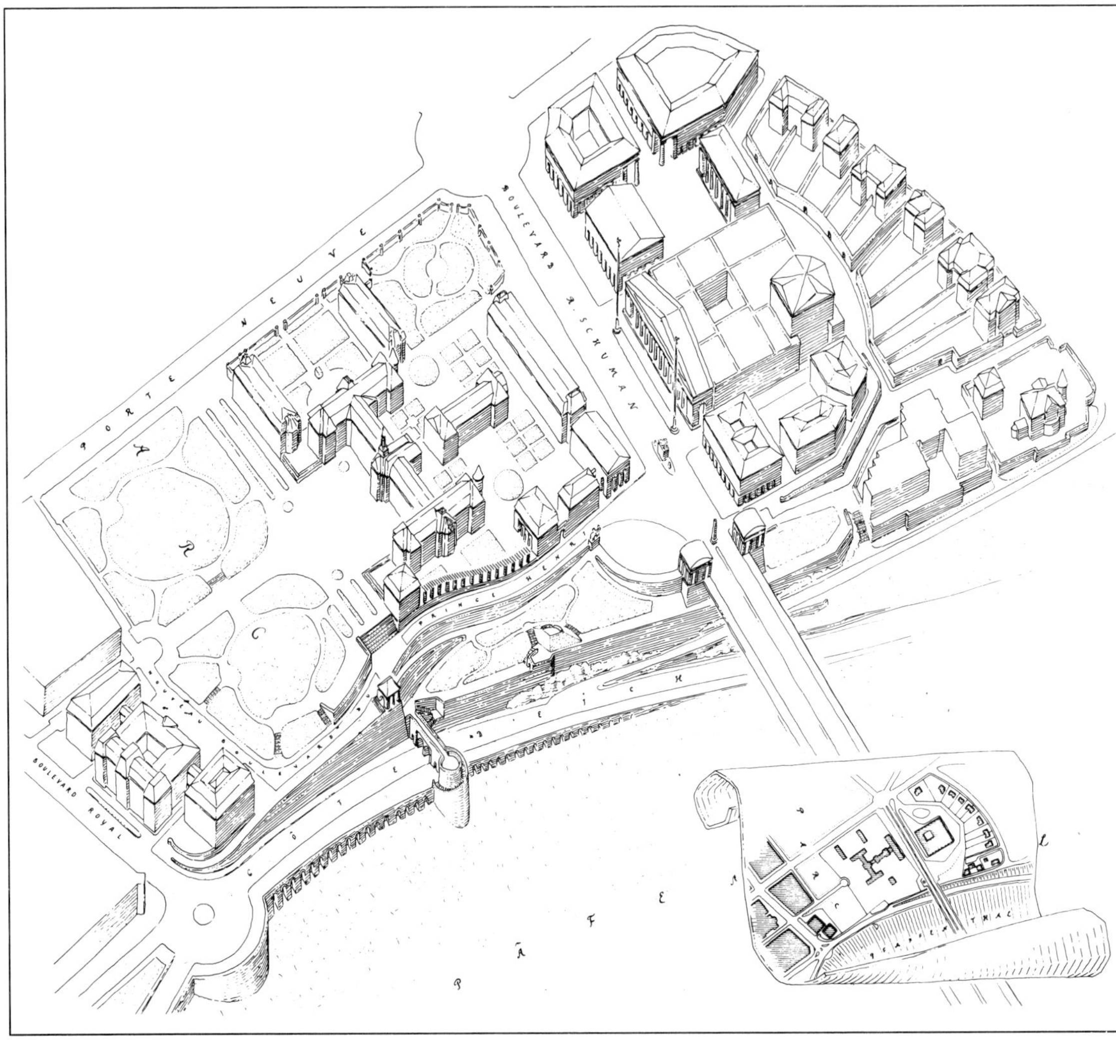

ABOVE: AERIAL VIEW; *BELOW*: PERSPECTIVE

The important institutions and organisations of the Grand Duchy regularly invite you to grace with your presence the inauguration of some building or structure. Putting aside all aesthetic considerations, this fine tradition cements the deep secular ties between the House of the Grand Duke and his people. In fact, building and maintaining cities and cultivating one's native land are unquestionably the supreme goals of any culture; building a beautiful homeland is the foremost duty of the fine arts and the ultimate objective of all judicious and wise sovereign powers. History shows us that with the passage of time it is not so much the individual artist who is remembered as the sovereign who marks an epoch or style with his personality and his vision. Thus it can be said that Louis XIV, Philip II and Frederick-William IV were the real architects of Versailles, the Escorial and Charlottenhof. In addition to such brilliant monuments, we also owe to the benevolence of sovereigns those great religious and secular structures which remain touchstones of profound value for our culture, despite the strident transformations of the machine age.

In addressing myself to you I am speaking not as the member of a profession or style, but as, dare I say, one who takes part in the centuries-old tradition of building cities. My profession has done too little of late by way of responding to the great demands made on it by the artistic traditions which have shaped our country and our continent. To tell the truth, your Royal Highness, the disfigurement of the Grand Duchy has caused me so much suffering that, as a patriot, I've had to exile myself from this country where the very principles and roots of my art are treated so thoughtlessly, with such cruel contempt.

The ideals of harmony, stability and utility found in Classical architecture are in accordance with the fundamental ideals of enduring human settlements, because for thousands of years the refined aesthetic, moral and technical qualities of this art have been the most noble means and indeed the preferred instrument for constituent powers to express the qualities of their civilisation . . . The artistic beauty and prestige of monuments is both the reflection and guarantee of the authority of the *res publica* itself.

Our industrial society is increasingly incapable of creating durable monuments and significant cultural events. Its impressive technological capabilities are but poor substitutes for the secular powers of Classical culture . . . A nation is made up not only of its people and history, but of all that one's look can encompass, all that one's senses can perceive. The forms of houses and grand buildings, of towns and landscapes, are the tangible expression of our values and morals. If we can no longer bring ourselves to love them, if they no longer inflame our hearts, they will force us to run away from them, to seek refuge in faraway countries, or even to lose ourselves in artificial paradises, in ghostly and unreal worlds.

In spite of the Grand Duchy being one of the most advanced industrial countries in the world, its powerful organisations have headquarters buildings which, with the exception of ARBED, can hardly be associated with any idea of beauty. In fact the country remains beautiful only in those corners which have managed to escape their grip. It seems to me that since the Duchy's millenium at least, the spectacular transformations that have taken place have succeeded only in impoverishing it: my colleagues in Luxembourg have made themselves the instruments of an economic policy devoid of any cultural vision. For architects brought up on a meagre diet of 'functionalism' and the 'International Style', taking care of one's country is a redundant and outmoded exercise, a value that is alien to them, an aim which is unknown. And yet man has always been made for a love of harmony. I'm not accusing any individual or group of bad faith here; rather I'd like to call on you, my Prince, to one day make your reign a source of moral and artistic inspiration, giving the builders of our cities and land the determination and courage they need to cultivate the beauty for which we shall always be indebted to them.

Leon Krier

*   *   *

The conviction that the entrance to a town deserves better than a mere technical calculation inspired the Government of the Grand Duchy to invite Rita Wolff and Leon Krier to make a proposal for reconstruction of the eastern flank of the rocky promontory on which the 1000-year-old city of Luxembourg is founded. In the past it was defended by a panoply of fortifications but the neutrality stipulated in the 1867 Treaty of London involved their dismantling. In their place, the Parisian garden architect André laid out a park bordered by boulevards, with only a few major avenues cutting through the new green belt, and a new access road, Cote d'Eich, was built along the flank of the valley giving access from the north. More recently a 300 metre-long bridge was built over Cote d'Eich and the Alzette valley to allow development of the Kirchberg plateau. An avenue links this to the old bridge Grande-Duchesse Charlotte at the Schuman circus. To the right of this entrance avenue is a theatre and an interesting row of rich urban villas, now mostly occupied by embassies and banks. The latest element is a tunnel under the old city, opened last summer.

Krier proposes to enhance the intersection of tunnel exit, boulevard entrance and Cote d'Eich by a big fountain in the centre of the recently built bastion. His plan shows the complex interaction of the various street-types built at different times and under difficult topographical conditions. It aims to exalt the character of each and add style to a rich historic site that in actuality has become very ordinary. He does not recommend the reconstruction of the fortress in a military style but rather rebuilding by an analogical approach some elements such as bastions, stone walls, towers and rampart walks, enriched by belvederes, view-points and pergolas.

Probably inspired by Joseph Stübben, who planned the neighbouring districts, Leon Krier adds some minor streets for the benefit of pedestrians and elongates the boulevard du Prince (to the south of the park) as far as the ramparts of Cote d'Eich. The new street follows the crest of these imposing stone walls until the old bridge. From here a pedestrian walk turns back down the ramparts to end up on a lower platform. A small picturesque bridge crosses the access road to reach a tower with external, encircling staircase and viewing point, which is founded on remains of the outermost defence walls. The pedestrian can then rejoin the pavements of the Cote d'Eich which have been lowered and ripped away from the noisy street.

The arches of the passerelle form a gateway to the town, an important element in the visual sequence for drivers. Next they will discover the fountain which brings into relief the first square *intra muros*. This also gives character to the entrance from Kirchberg, one level above. At the end of the huge Grande-Duchesse Charlotte bridge are two pavilions either side of the abutment and an obelisk between the two traffic lines. An imposing gallery of edifices leads the progression to the Schuman circus, establishing a real entrance avenue and culminating in the view of the great column at its centre.

Bernard Neis

THE TOWER

ARNDT, MALMQUIST AND SKOOGH
Bryggaren, Stockholm

The recently completed Bryggaren project incorporates a new office building flanked by two small restored 19th-century buildings. The new building is meant to be a new link in the long chain of Stockholm Classicism. The composition holds reminiscences of both the mid-19th century (a thriving period for Stockholm) when a light, French-inspired architecture predominated, as in the Stock Exchange Building, and the architecture of the 1920s, for example the headquarters for Swedish Match, low-key, discreet but very distinctive.

On the restored building the original 1880s entrance had been demolished in the 30s leaving only the original staircase, so the entrance is new in every detail, except for the staircase, which in the true Viollet-le-Duc manner has been 'reconstructed to a shape it never had'. Marble, plaster and decorative painting were used in a way that was new for me and the result was somewhat different to what I had anticipated – the perspective is milder, a bit more Pre-Raphaelite perhaps.

If the street facade draws its inspiration from local Classicism, the quotations of the courtyard have a wider European background: Schinkel, Stüler, mid-Victorian buildings like Bunning's London Coal Exchange (long since gone). The materials are simple: plaster, concrete, wood and iron. The glass roof of the courtyard gives protection against a harsh climate. It also gives you a vision of a more comfortable world, the eternal northern longing for a Mediterranean world. The *volière* of the perspective was subsituted by a small cast-iron fountain (nice for the birds!). The huge porticoed window gives side-light, which is important as in a narrow glazed-in courtyard, a glass roof somehow tends to strengthen the well-like feeling if daylight only enters from above.

The facades with narrow balconies are new. The plain facade of the remaining building has been decorated – in converting what was once just a service backyard into something between a courtyard and an interior, I felt that more than a plain wall was needed.

The original top of the tower was demolished during the crucial years around 1930. The new one is a free reconstruction, using the original mansard styling in a 20th-century interpretation, crowned by wrought-iron lacework. The facade was also brutally simplified in 1930, I tried to give it enough detailing to make the original overall composition legible.

Thomas Malmquist

COURTYARD, NEW BUILDING AND FOUNTAIN

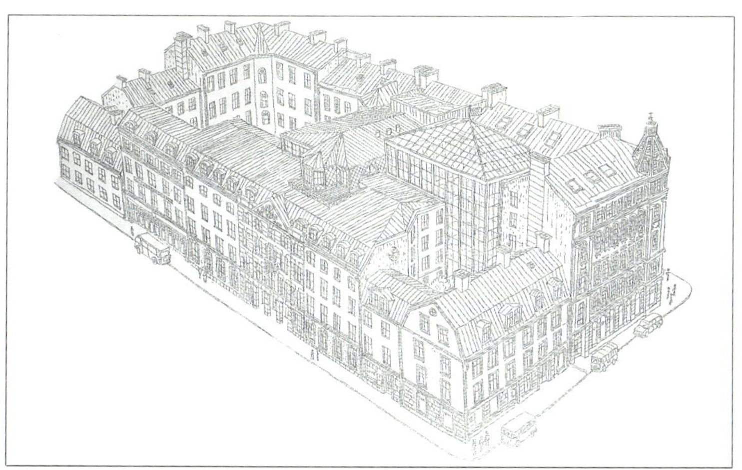

ABOVE L TO R: PERSPECTIVE DRAWING; STAIRWAY; *CENTRE L TO R*: SHOP FRONT; OLD BUILDING, DECORATED COURTYARD FACADE; *BELOW*: STREET FACADE

DIETER BAUMEWERD
Billerbeck Housing Project

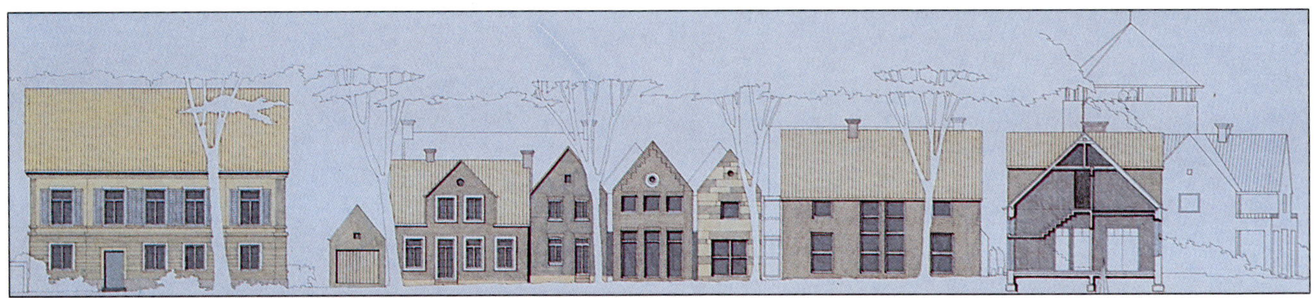

CHURCH SQUARE, BILLERBECK, *ABOVE*: EAST SIDE; *CENTRE*: VIEW FROM EAST; *BELOW*: NORTH SIDE

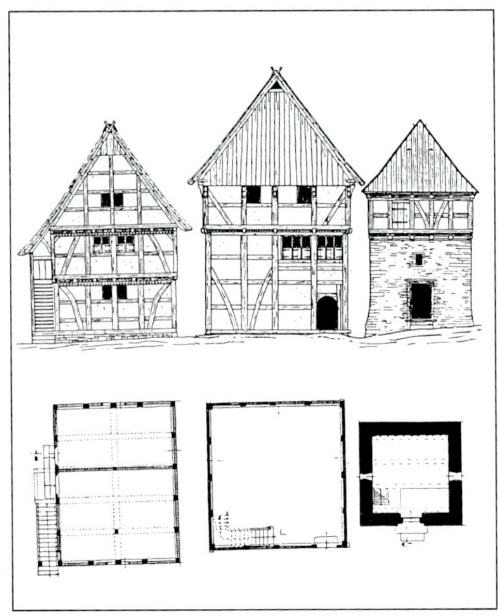

VERNACULAR HOUSING TYPES

The *Speicherhäuser* around the Cathedral in Billerbeck were built by farmers over a long span of time. They contained storage on the ground floor for the produce that had to be brought to the nearby market, with living quarters above. Modern farming practice, however, made these *Speicherhäuser* redundant and they were abandoned in the 1960s, steadily declining ever since.

The task here was to convert them into flats for the elderly and single-parent families, retaining as much of the existing historic fabric as possible, and to provide additional family housing in a complementary style. The new buildings draw on local precedent for the forms of the houses and roofs, the choice of materials and detailing.

Assistants: Lukas & Benedikt Baumewerd

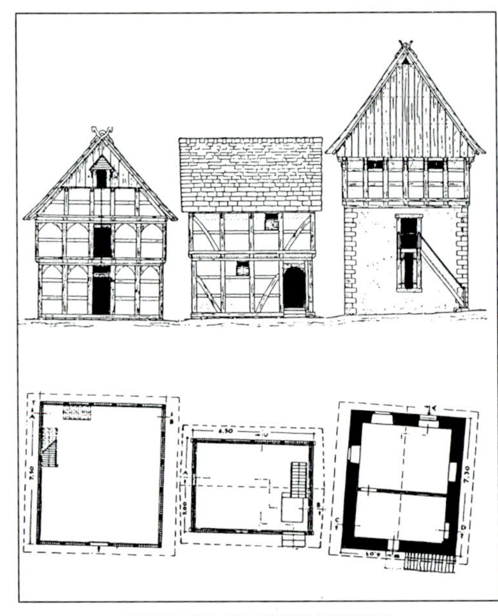

VERNACULAR HOUSING TYPES

MARK HEWITT
Country House at Peacock Point, Long Island

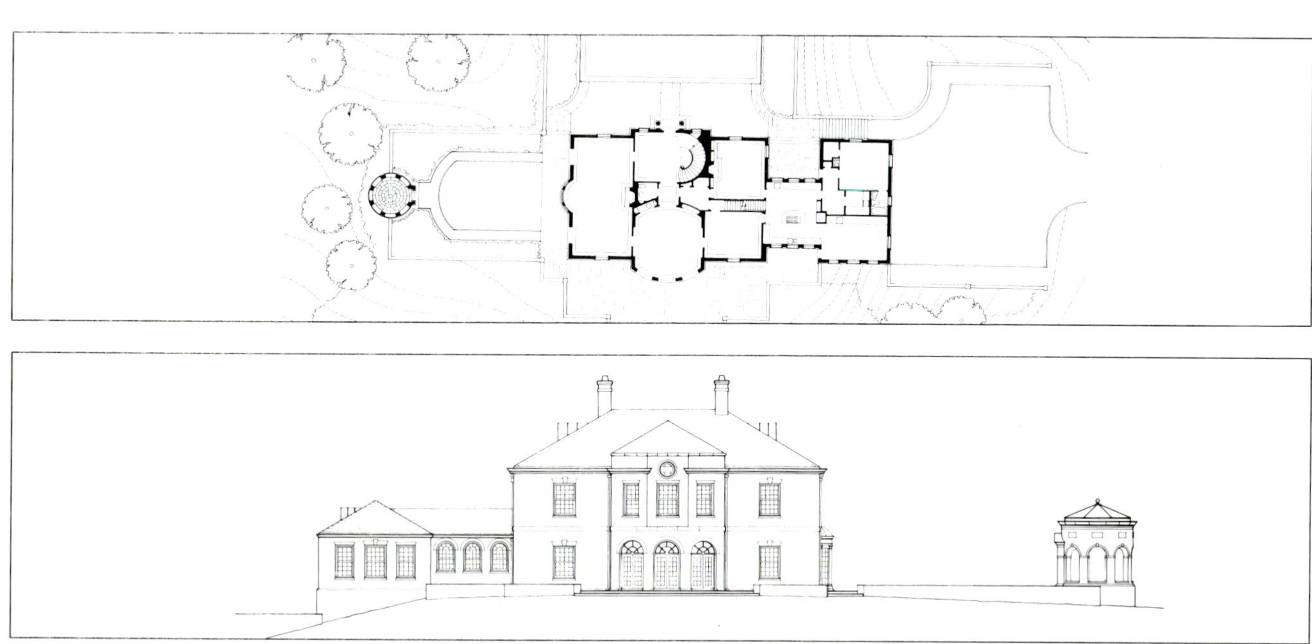

ABOVE: SITE PLAN; *CENTRE*: NORTH ELEVATION; *BELOW*: SOUTH ELEVATION

With views over the water from its hilltop site, this family house was designed to satisfy both an Anglophile desire for an English Georgian house on a formal circuit plan and the American penchant for relaxation and functional ease.

The models chosen were a hybrid of English 18th-century and American colonial revival sources: John Soane, Robert Adam, William Adams Delano, Mott B Schmidt and the nearby houses, John Russell Pope's Caumsett and Grosvenor Atterbury's Old Westbury. The result is pared-down Georgian with attention given to details: large, handmade bricks, bold cornice, the Ionic aedicular doorway based on Palladio. Yet within the imitation, Classical models are also reinterpreted to give new juxtapositions – the split pediments marked by a circular *oeil de boeuf* motif tie together the central units of the pedimented south facade and the bow-front of the north facade; whilst an association is made between the space of the living room on the west side and the adjacent walled garden, through the use of two facing 'temples', one a bow window of Federal inspiration, the other a circular, brick Temple of the Winds, loosely based on Gibbs.

In several key respects our approach to this design used imitation. In fact to the untutored eye, the plan and image of the house are so familiar as to seem almost archetypal. That is the intention. Domestic architecture is implicitly conservative – this Georgian house especially so, for much as 18th-century furniture demands a high level of connoisseurship, so does this style dèmand a level of refinement and reserve that cannot be appreciated without a cultivated eye.

GARDEN TEMPLE

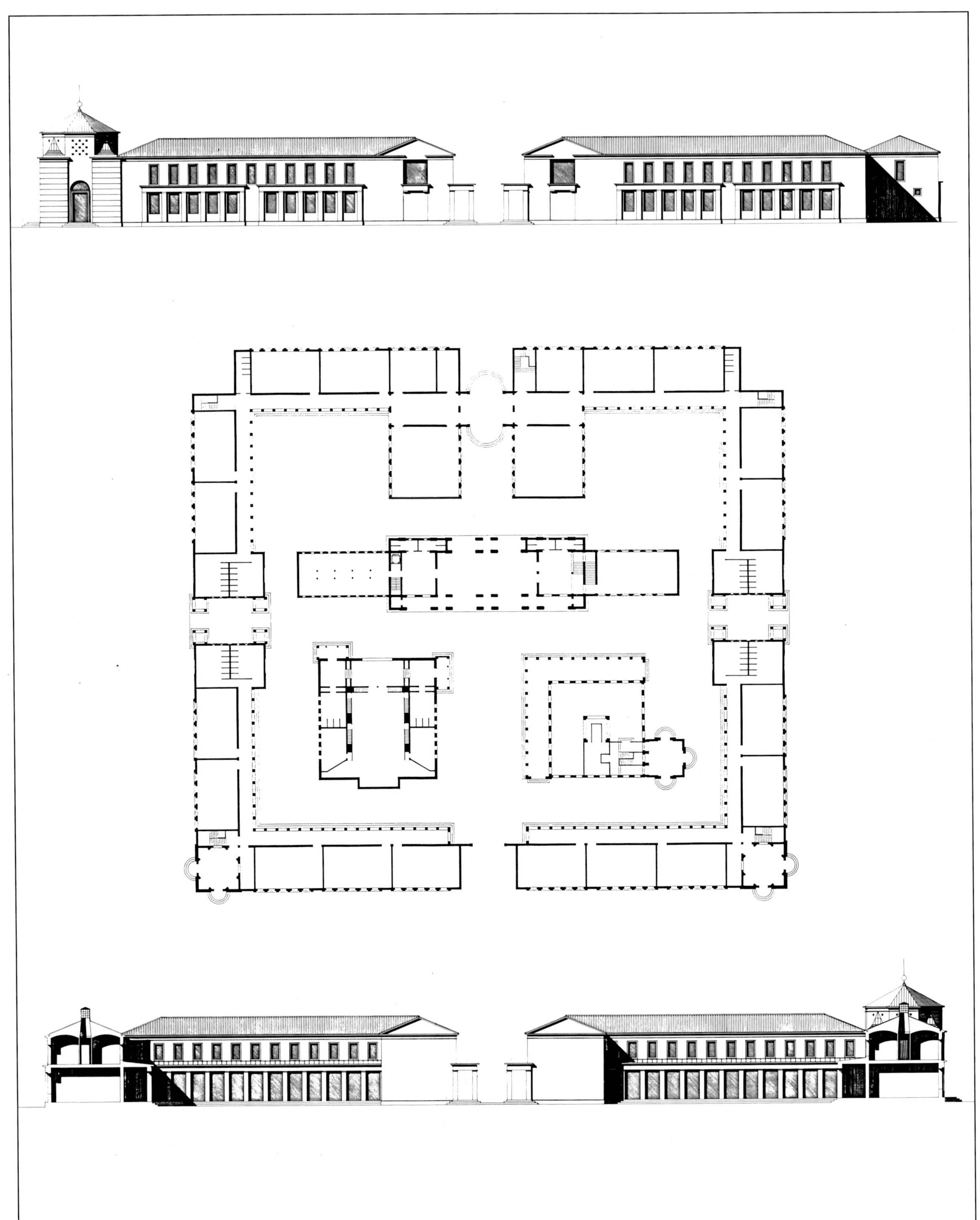

ABOVE: EXTERIOR FACADE; *CENTRE*: GROUND-FLOOR PLAN; *BELOW*: INTERIOR FACADE

INIGUEZ AND USTARROZ
Faculty Building at the University of the Basque Country

ABOVE: COURT WITH AULA MAGNA, LIBRARY AND DEAN'S LODGE; *BELOW*: PLAN OF UNIVERSITY CAMPUS

The site specified for the Faculty of Philosophy, Education and Psychology was a block of 109 x 97 metres. The Senate of the Faculty desired, on the one hand, to establish the independence of the three departments, with their own lecture halls, seminar rooms and professors' offices, and on the other, the construction of communal buildings for the whole faculty.

Starting from this basis, the architecture of the new buildings refers to the best traditions of university buildings from all times and places – it is said that buildings arranged around a central space, courtyard or cloister have a unified ambience, a characteristic we could recall in the beautiful examples of Salamanca and Alcala and also in any European city from Oxford to Cambridge, Pavia to Cracow, without forgetting the Jeffersonian University of Virginia in America.

These principles seemed to give the right conditions and led to the main design proposals of our plan, in an architectural language that was rigorous yet still allowed a great variety of combinations. Firstly, a grand cloister or interior court, bounded by independent buildings for philosophy, education and psychology.

Secondly, the lateral buildings are of two-storeys, broken by entrances to the grand court from outside. Each departmental building is organised typologically in the same way – on the ground floor are various lecture halls and services in a linear arrangement linked by the arcaded *galeria* that is a unifying element of all the courtyard elevations. On the first floor are professors' offices and seminar rooms. Mention must also be made of the octagonal, triple space in the departments of philosophy and education lit at the top

through pierced walls that give an impression of transparency.

Thirdly, the communal elements inside the court, which are seen to symbolise the faculty. The Aula Magna (Grand Hall) is modelled on the Greek *bouleuterion*. It is square in plan and seats 500. From the outside it looks like a huge, brick cube with pyramidal roof, animated by two small porticos towards street and court. The four-storey Dean's Lodge faces the Aula Magna, and occupies the same floor area. The Library is a large, long building in three sections, two side wings hold book stacks and study rooms and a central part conceived as a bridge between the two gives access on the ground floor to the court and the books. Above it, the grand lecture room is a double-height space with balconies and tall windows on the upper level.

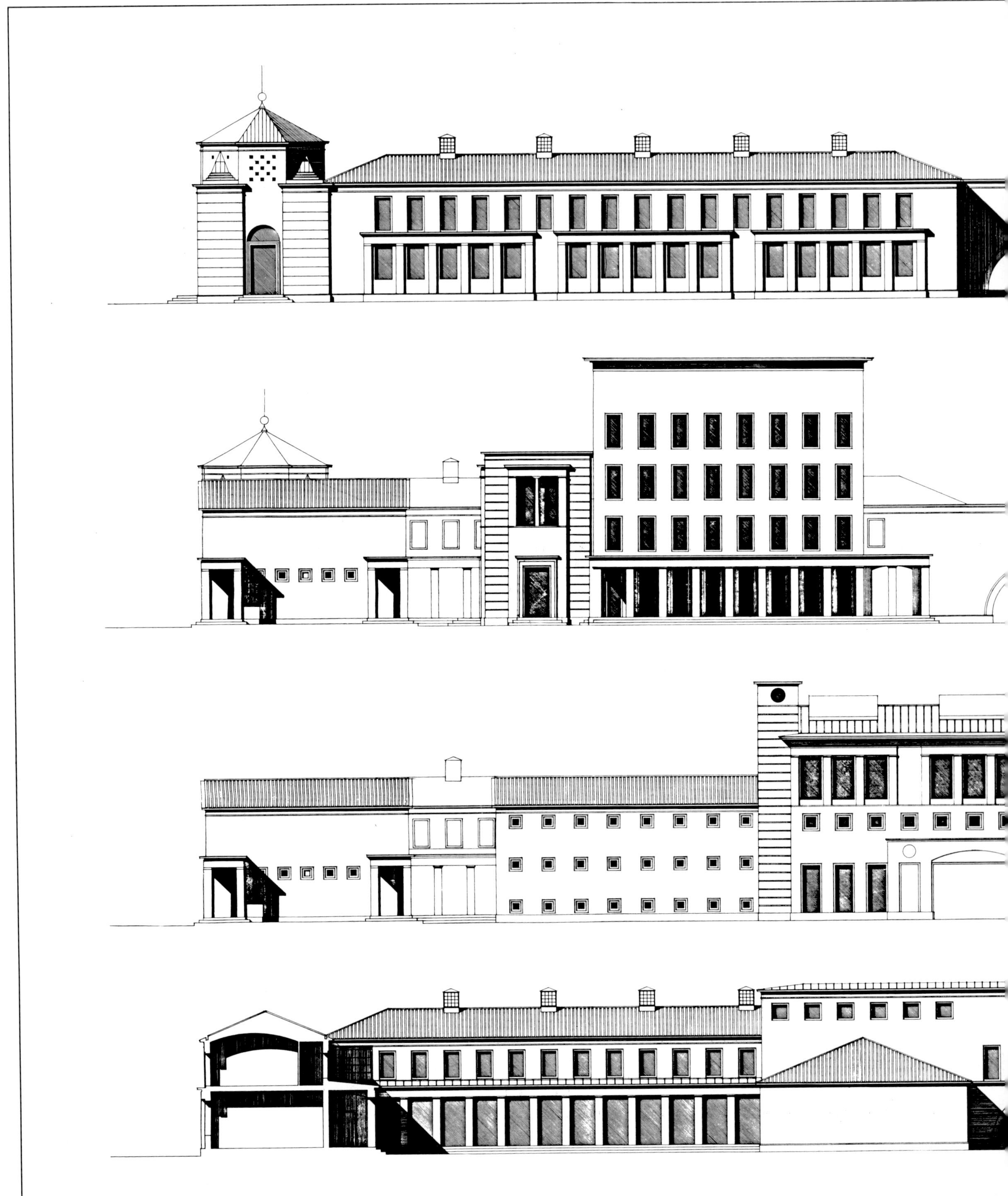

FROM TOP: DEPARTMENTS OF PHILOSOPHY AND EDUCATION; DEA

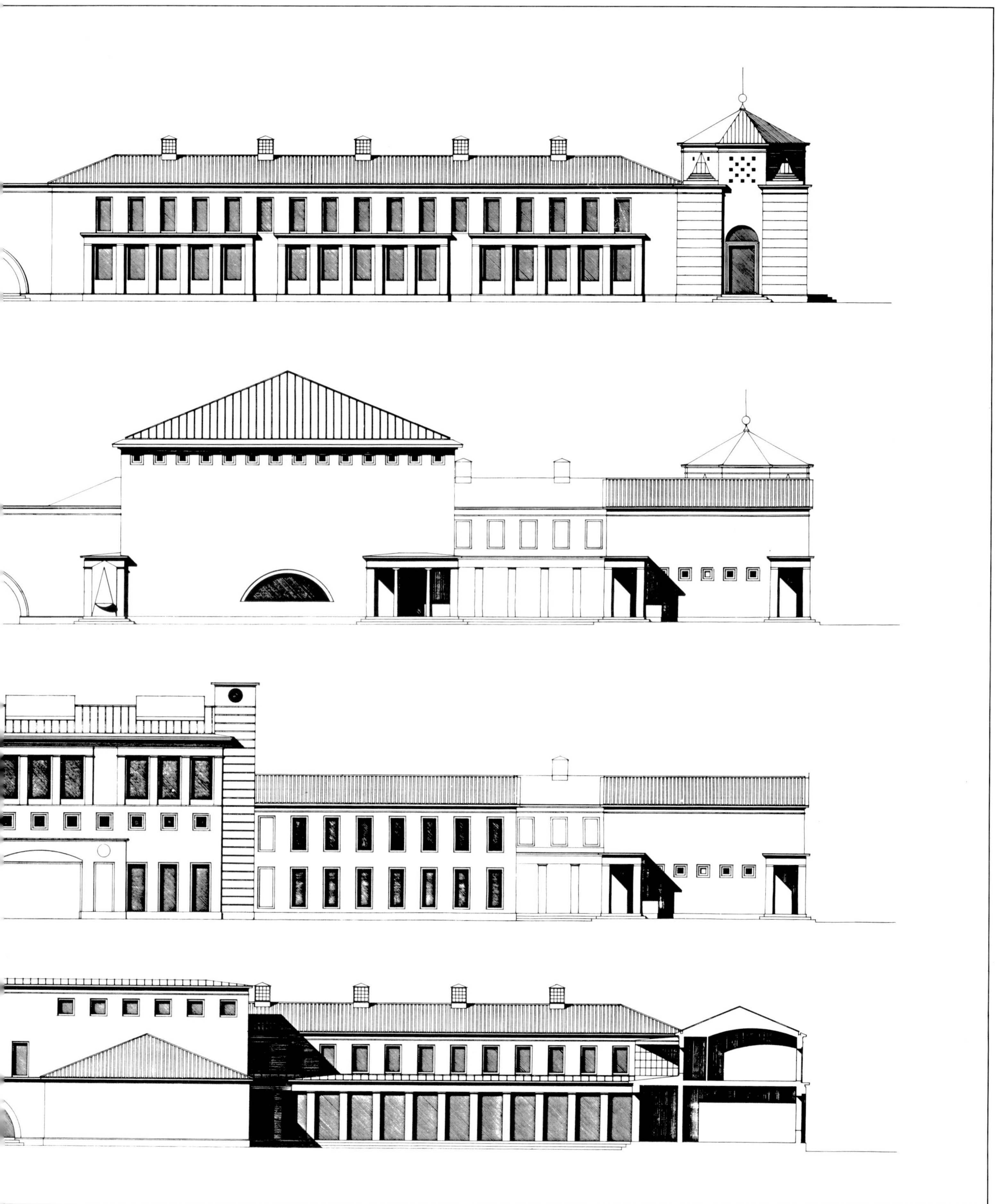

ODGE AND AULA MAGNA; LIBRARY; DEPARTMENT OF PSYCHOLOGY

MULTI-PURPOSE BUILDING, COLONNADE

HAMMOND BEEBY AND BABKA
Hole-in-the-Wall Gang Camp, Connecticut

DINING HALL

This camp for children with cancer and other life threatening illnesses was founded by Paul Newman to provide a full outdoor experience for those who would normally be denied that possibility by the nature of their physical condition. The environment is intended to remove campers from their daily experience that is often crushing and relentless and suspend them momentarily in another world.

The project was thus designed to incorporate all the elements of a community in miniature and its site plan has been based on historical plans of the traditional American small town. The individual building elements are intended to represent the various communal and private functions of such a settlement: dining hall, meeting place and the cabins where the children sleep.

Gravel paths, many of them built over existing farm and logging roads, traverse the site. Children pass between activities on foot or, where physically necessary, on small electric carts. Automobiles are excluded from the camp and service is accomplished on a separate road system shielded from the pedestrian precinct. The arrangement of the camp is based on a cinemagraphic unfolding of space and buildings, that recalls images of rural and frontier settlements. Figural buildings seen along controlled vistas serve as landmarks to inform campers and orient them in their daily routine.

The idea of community is suggested by the major spaces that define the camp. The town centre is a green bounded by major public buildings, comprised of the dining hall, gym and meeting room. A street formed by the facades of the craft shops, commissary and dispensary connects the green with the campers' cabins. Directors' houses mark the gates that lead to the cabin settlement. Cabins are grouped in clusters of three around a circular ceremonial space. A linear clearing between abandoned stone walls connects the cabins to the hemlock forest and the brook. Recreational facilities are spatially linked to the central focus of the lake.

The architecture attempts to provide a setting that speaks to the continuum of American vernacular building traditions from first settlement until today. It is meant to be experienced in an immediate and physical way in order to be legible to children. Every attempt has been made to overcome any reference to the medical origin of the institution that ultimately is its reason for being. Here children will hopefully be able to imagine themselves in a world free both in time and space.

BOAT HOUSE AND PIER

BATH HOUSE AND SWIMMING POOL.

ABOVE: INTERIOR; BELOW L TO R: EAST FACADE; WEST FACADE

CENICACELAYA AND SALOÑA
Rural Centre at La Rigada, Muskiz

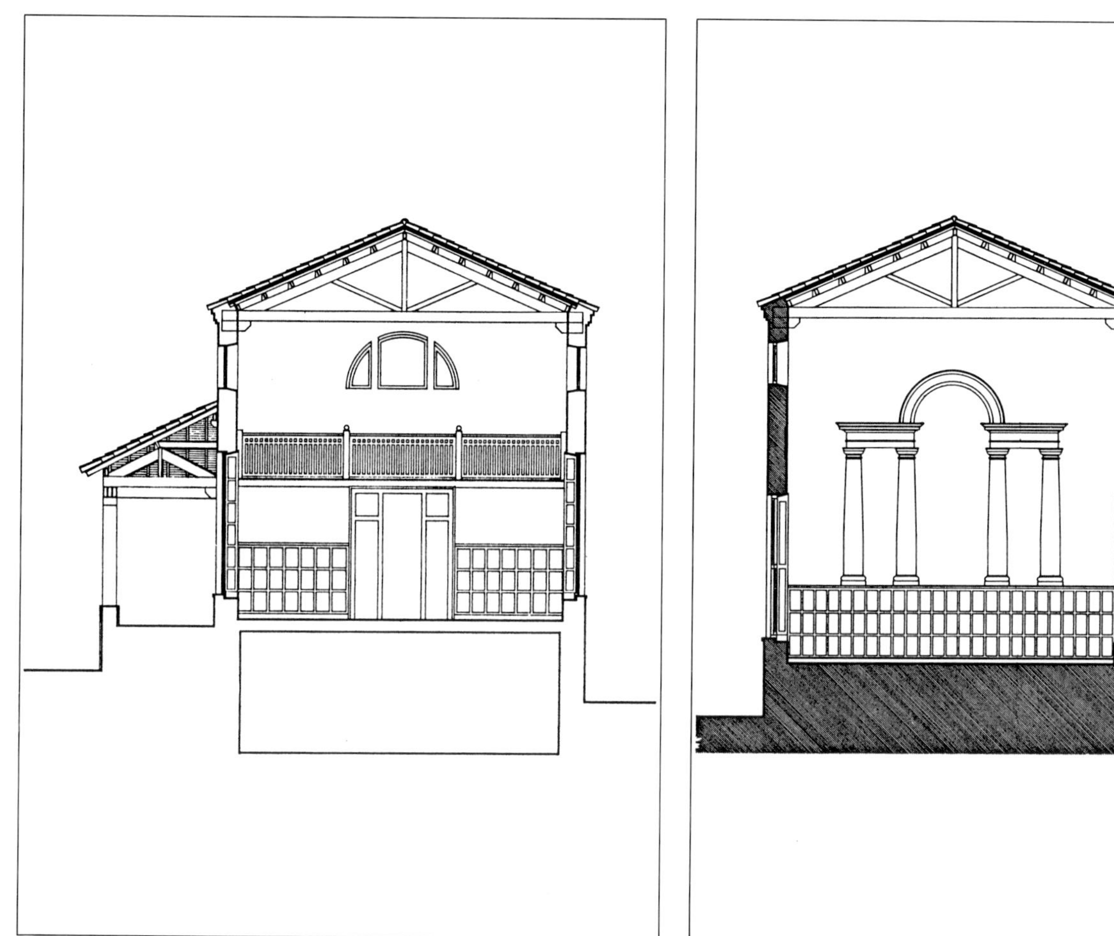

TRANSVERSE SECTIONS

The Rural Centre (1985-7) is a small building where a number of different activities can take place: cinema, theatre, meetings, lectures, etc. It thus operates as the social meeting point and centre for the small, rural, farming village of La Rigada, in Muskiz.

The building is located close to a *campa* or plain open space, used as the meeting area of the community in different outdoor celebrations throughout the year, and close to the local church, which has a pelota court (a ball game that in the villages of the Basque country is particularly associated with the church) attached to it.

We decided to design a 'hall' to establish a linkage with the long tradition of this building typology in the Atlantic cultures, and to give us the form which allows for the greatest variety of activities and functions. The principal room is the large meeting hall, but there are also cloakrooms and a lower-level changing room (entered at the east end) for the pelota players.

This is a building which appears symmetrical but where in fact each facade is different in its function and character. The 'hall' is surrounded on three sides by a portico of 17 Tuscan columns (the most rural of the orders) facing the *campa* and the pelota court on the south and west sides, and to the east facing on to a beautiful view of the rural landscape. The portico is distinguished on the west side where it is of double width as befits the entrance facade. The north side lacks a portico as a small track and the proximity to the steep hillside did not make it suitable.

The building has been conceived in a vernacular way and using local materials. The columns of the portico are of white limestone and stand on a rubble-work stone platform of the same material, raising the hall above the level of the *campa*, the walls are in stuccoed brick, the tiled roof is supported on a traditional wooden structure, the paving is in clay.

In the interior of the building the walls are covered by wooden panelling. The tall sash windows are provided with shutters, that remain hidden, folded into the walls. One enters, at the west end, on the ground floor under the choir gallery which is designed in the traditional manner, a continuous piece of dovetailed wood with perforations to obtain transparency. Extra light is provided by the Palladian window at the east end, a thermal window high above the choir and by high eye-hole windows on the side walls which also add to the compositional quality of the facades.

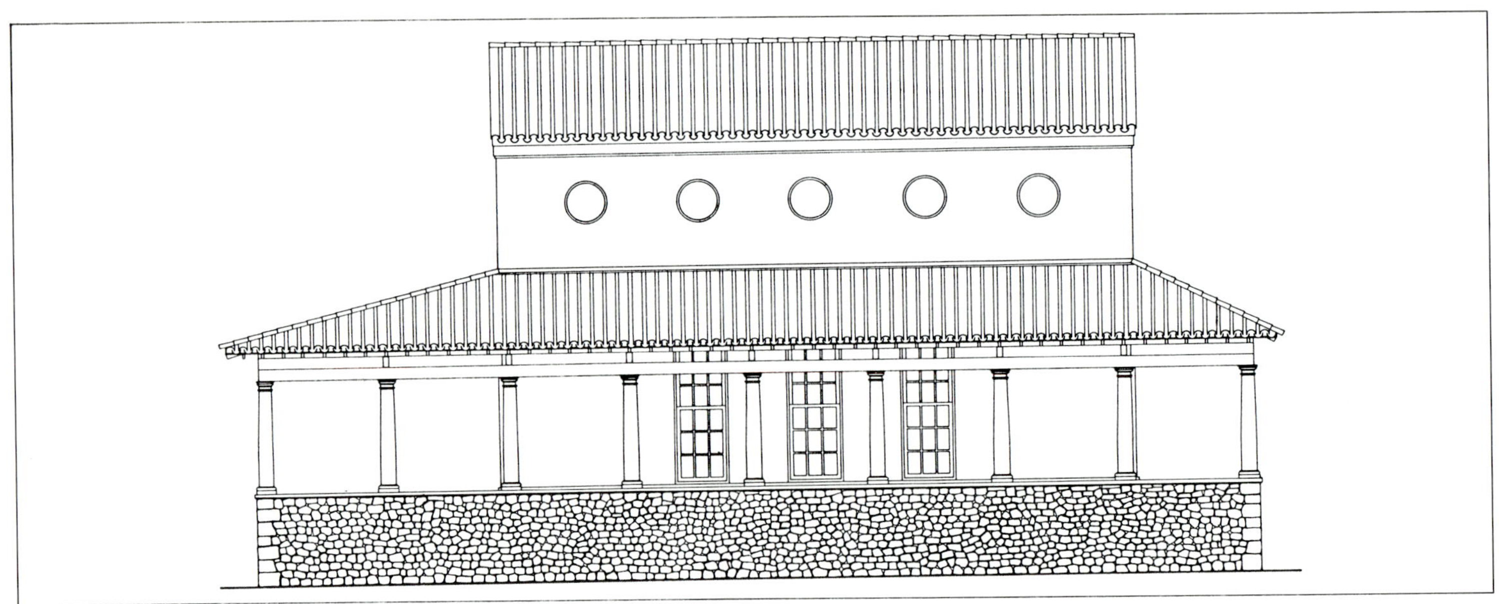

ABOVE: VIEW FROM SOUTHWEST; *BELOW*: SOUTH ELEVATION

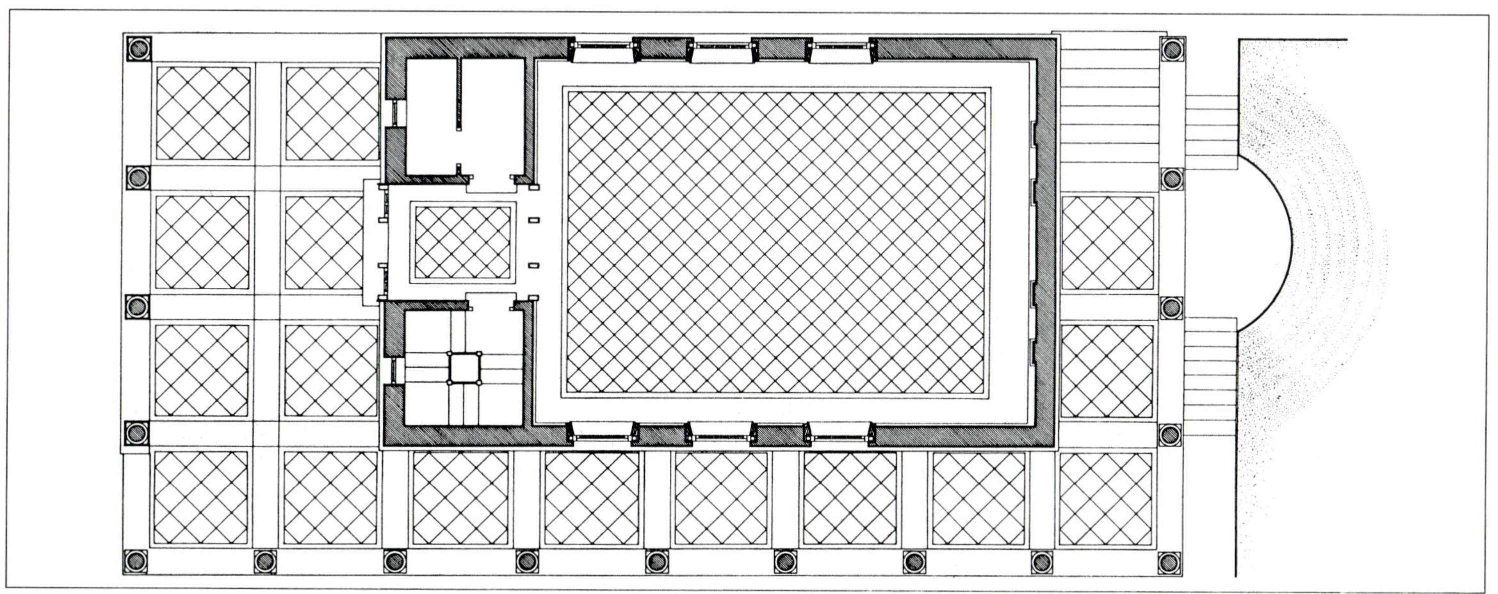

ABOVE: VIEW FROM NORTHWEST; BELOW: FLOOR PLAN

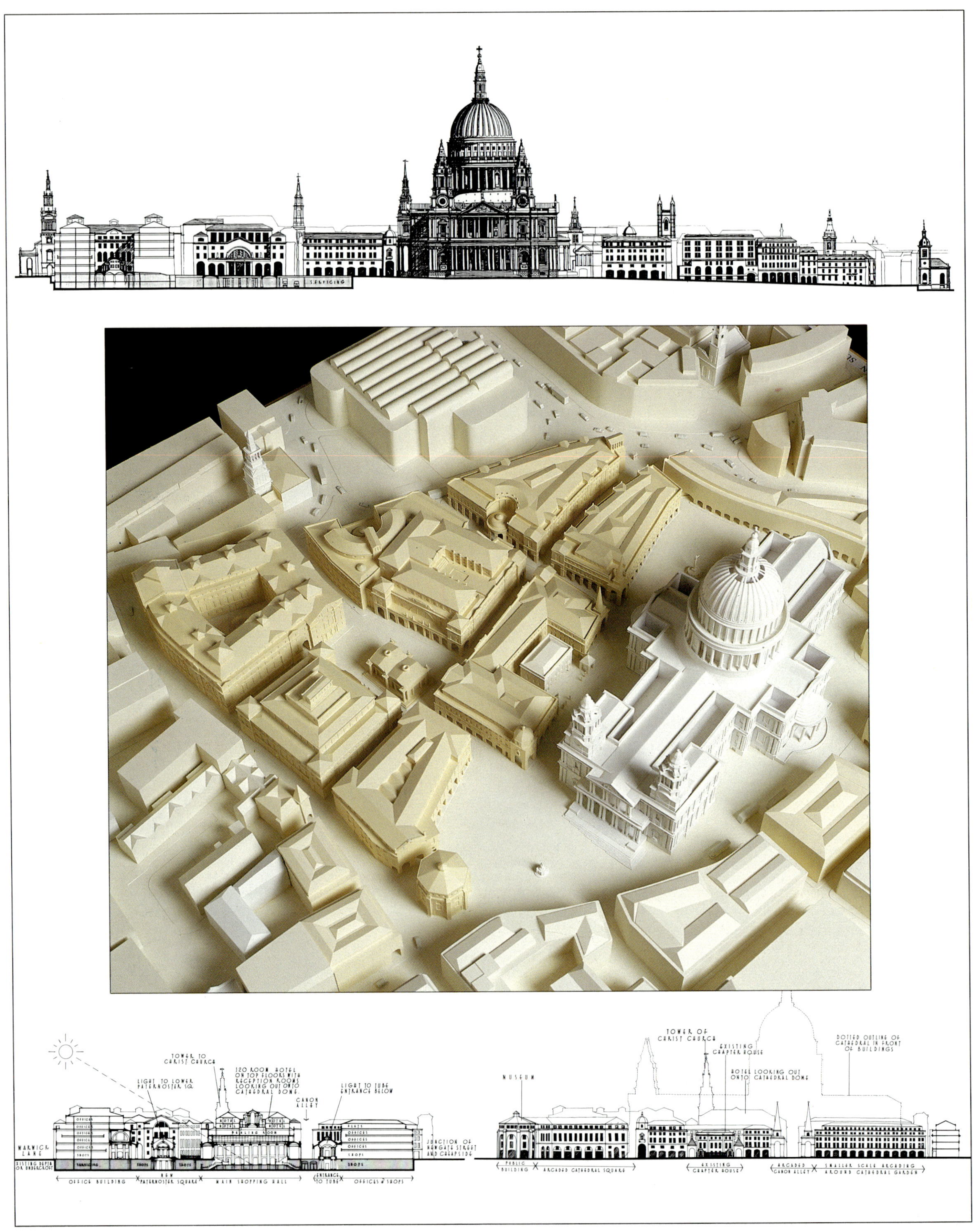

ABOVE: COMPARISON OF NEW BLOCKS TO ST PAUL'S AND CITY CHURCHES; *CENTRE*: GENERAL VIEW OF MODEL; *BELOW L TO R*: SECTION; ELEVATION

JOHN SIMPSON
Paternoster Square Redevelopment Project

This issue at Paternoster Square is how St Paul's is to relate to the rest of the City fabric. It would be common sense therefore to start with the cathedral at the centre of the masterplan and develop a strategy for the whole surrounding area.

The area to the southwest that survived the bombing and 60s redevelopment gives a good indication of the setting for which Wren designed his cathedral. All the special buildings exist but are stranded out of context. To recreate a sensible relationship between these buildings, the obvious place to begin is the old prewar street pattern. We have modified this as the original narrow streets were laid out when three or four storeys were commonplace not the five or six proposed today. The area around old Paternoster Square was also unnecessarily intricate for modern-day usage. To integrate the development

more gradually into the City as it is today the block sizes furthest from the cathedral have been enlarged to correspond with postwar London. Around St Paul's however medieval size and scale is vital. The cathedral's architectural presence would be reinforced by contrast with small utilitarian buildings and the dramatic views so characteristic of its old setting would be created along intricate narrow lanes between these blocks.

No one can deny that content and density play a vital part in the character of an area. It is important that there is a sufficient mix of uses for the regeneration of genuine urban life around the cathedral with the streets and squares normal to a traditional city. The plan must also capitalise on the richness and diversity of a group of buildings by different designers but must select architects sympathetic to

the masterplan design, not a diverse range of architects from High Tech to Classical by which we would attain an identical mess in every city. True pluralism requires us to maintain the individuality and character of each of our towns and cities; St Paul's must have a traditional setting.

Finally, to accuse anyone building in a traditional Classical style of merely trying to rebuild the past is to misunderstand the nature of tradition. No one would dispute that Wren's design for St Paul's was modern for its day. Similarly a Classical architect today is drawing on a cultural inheritance thousands of years old. It is the Modern Movement which is in fact perpetrating redundant ideas from the late 19th and early 20th centuries. It is because I do not desire to reproduce the past that I design traditional buildings.

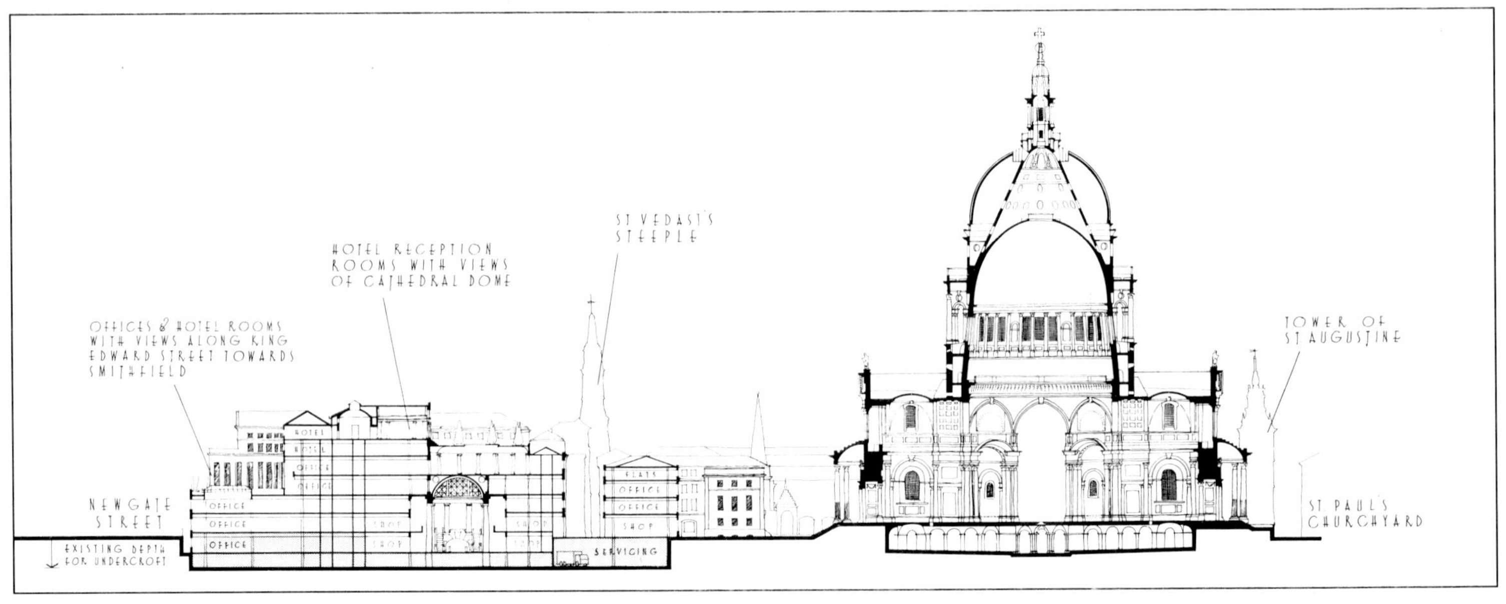

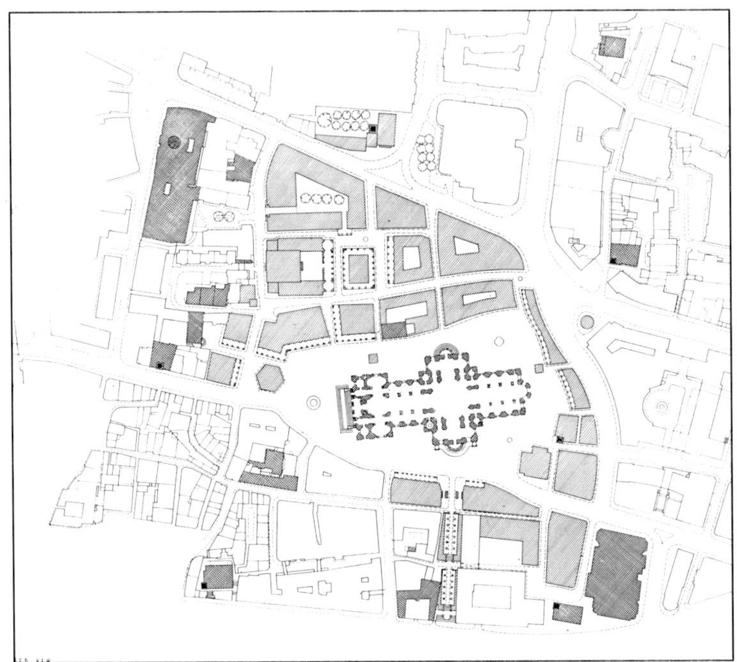

ABOVE: SECTION; *CENTRE L TO R*: SITE PLAN, INTERIOR OF BASILICA; *BELOW L TO R*: PATERNOSTER SQUARE; VIEW OF ST PAUL'S; VIEW FROM DEAN'S COURT